THINGS I NEVER LEARNED IN SUNDAY SCHOOL

Facts About the Christian Faith That Will Surprise and Astound You

Nan Yielding

Writing ... Etc.
Oregon, U.S.A.
www.writing-etc.com

"If you're going to put all your faith into something, you need to thoroughly examine it to make sure your faith is justified."

–Unknown

Copyright © 2012 by Nan Yielding

All rights reserved. This book may not be reproduced in whole or in part by any means, electronic, mechanical, photocopying, or recording without written permission from the publisher, except by a reviewer who may quote brief passages in a review or as provided under Fair Use provisions outlined by the U.S. Copyright Law. Inquiries should be addressed to publish@writing-etc.com

Editorial: Tracy Hart (editingwithhart.com)

Cover design: Susan Johnson (partner4success.com)

Unless otherwise indicated, all scripture quotations in this book are taken from the NEW REVISED STANDARD VERSION BIBLE, Copyright 1989 by the Division of Christian Education of the National Council of Churches of Christ in the U.S.A., and are used by permission. All rights reserved.

Scriptures marked NIV are taken from the Holy Bible, NEW INTERNATIONAL VERSION®, Copyright 1973, 1978, 1984 by Biblica, Inc.™ Used by permission. All rights reserved worldwide.

Scriptures marked ASV are taken from the NEW AMERICAN STANDARD BIBLE®, Copyright 1960,1962,1963,1968,1971,1972,1973,1975,1977,1995 by The Lockman Foundation. Used by permission.

Scriptures marked (NLT) are taken from the Holy Bible, NEW LIVING TRANSLATION, Copyright 1996, 2004, 2007 by Tyndale House Foundation. Used by permission of Tyndale House Publishers, Inc., Carol Stream, Illinois 60188. All rights reserved.

Scriptures marked NKJV are taken from the Holy Bible, NEW KING JAMES VERSION®, Copyright © 1982 by Thomas Nelson, Inc. Used by permission. All rights reserved.

Scriptures marked KVJ are taken from the AUTHORIZED KING JAMES VERSION, which is public domain in the United States.

ISBN: 978-1-930470-05-7

TABLE OF CONTENTS

Acknowledgments i

Preface 1

Introduction 7

1. THE BIBLE: More Than Meets the Eye 9

2. JESUS: Messiah? Savior? God? 25

3. JESUS: Second Time Around 37

4. PAUL: A Man With a Mission 47

5. THE BIG BAD GUY: Is He For Real? 67

6. HELL: How Hot Is It? 89

7. END TIMES: Famines, Earthquakes, Wars ... Oh My! 107

8. ANTICHRIST: The Master Deceiver 117

9. GOD: The X Factor 125

Epilogue 141

Resources 143

Appendix 149

Selected Reading 151

Endnotes 153

ACKNOWLEDGMENTS

There were several individuals who played a role in bringing this book to fruition and I extend my heartfelt gratitude to each of them:

Tracy Hart, my book coach/editor who provided ongoing encouragement and inspiration, and who challenged me when writer's block threatened to rear its ugly head.

Jeff Maziarek, a self-published author who provided guidance and direction in the publishing process, as well as suggestions and changes to the first draft manuscript.

Michael Yielding, my life's partner for his support, patience, and understanding.

Susan Johnson, an extremely talented graphic designer who created the unique book cover.

Chris Chidester, a good friend and spiritual ally who provided much food for thought related to the contents of the book.

Clark Minor, my son and a dedicated Christian who provided feedback on the first draft manuscript.

Jeremy Nehf, a friend and Christian pastor who shared his perspective in the beginning stages of the book.

PREFACE

"Many people live their entire lives simply accepting what others have told them."
–David N. Elkins, Ph.D., Beyond Religion[1]

"Do not ask questions; just believe."
–Celsus, 2nd Century Greek Philosopher/Writer

This book was born out of my disillusionment and disappointment with the Christian religion. Although I spent fifteen years as a devoted, dedicated (and often fervent) Christian, there came a time when I began to feel like my Christian experience was more about living up to the doctrines of the church than it was on developing a deeper relationship with God. I longed to feel more love and less fear.

I became a "born again" Christian when I was in my early twenties. It was a very major and dramatic event for me because up until that time, I had not been at all religious. I wasn't raised in church and, in fact, had only been inside a church building on three or four occasions during my lifetime. It wasn't that I didn't believe in God. I was just indifferent to and uninterested in religious matters.

Once I invited Jesus into my life, however, everything changed. My life, quite literally, did a 180 degree turn. I immersed myself in the Bible, prayed daily, enthusiastically shared my newfound faith with others, attended church services without fail, became active in the choir, taught Sunday School, and helped with Vacation Bible School. I even became church secretary for a short time. In other words, I identified with what Paul wrote in Philippians 1:21, *For to me, living is Christ ...*

The church I attended held to very conservative evangelical beliefs. Besides teaching that the Bible is the literal and inerrant word of God, they also had strict views on how Christians should live – no drinking, no smoking, no dancing, no movies, no card-playing, no "mixed bathing." Women were expected to dress conservatively and refrain from wearing makeup or jewelry. (Of course, no such constraints or dress codes were imposed on the men.) "Worldly" music was unacceptable and to be avoided. In other words, any resemblance to what most people would consider normal living was forbidden. All of these restrictions were based on the church's interpretation of Bible scripture.

From the very beginning, I accepted these and other doctrines of the church without question. After all, I was a neophyte when it came to Christianity. Who was I to question what others so obviously knew more about than me? Only years later did I realize that I was placing my spiritual life in someone else's hands by not searching the scriptures for myself.

A Subliminal Shift

I can't pinpoint the exact moment when I started to feel different about my Christian experience; it was a very gradual process. One of the first things I recall is asking myself how following the strict rules and regulations of the church would help me draw closer to God. I also began to wonder why there was so much emphasis on sin and guilt instead of God's love.

Then I began noticing the judgmental attitude exhibited by some of the more "respected" members of the congregation. This probably disturbed me more than anything. Didn't Jesus say not to judge? And didn't the Bible say that God looks on the heart?

As time passed, I began to reflect upon other things: Is Jesus truly the *only* way to God? How can we be sure the Bible is "God's Word"? Is there really a "hell"? Where did the idea of Satan come from? If God is omnipresent, why are we taught that He lives somewhere "up there"? And why is God always referred to as a male?

Occasionally, I would turn to church leaders for answers, but invariably, all they would do is quote scripture or tell me to "pray about it." In other words, as Celsus wrote, "Do not ask questions; just believe."

This wasn't enough. I wanted to know the whys and wherefores behind the beliefs I had faithfully lived by for so many years.

Finally I realized I would have to go outside the church to find answers, so I started reading books on spirituality and religion. One of the first books I picked up was *Return to Love* by Marianne Williamson. The title alone spoke to my heart because this is what my soul was searching for. As I added other books to my reading list, I noticed I was experiencing more and more "A-ha" moments. I began to see that a person could be spiritual, but not religious. My excitement was growing.

More to Explore

Over time my search for understanding gathered momentum and I began reading more scholarly works, including books about the historical Jesus, the origin of the bible, the beginnings of Christianity, the birth of Satan, among others. (A complete bibliography is provided at the end of this book.)

In addition, I spent countless hours on the internet, pored over magazine articles, and studied several religious documentaries presented by the *History Channel*, the *Discovery Channel*, *PBS*, *CNN*, and others. I also met with members of the clergy and had probing discussions with practicing Christians, as well as those outside the Christian faith. The more information I absorbed, the more I realized the beliefs that had kept me living under a shadow of guilt and fear were not part of Jesus' teachings. Rather, they came from surrounding cultures and had been incorporated into the Jewish belief system long before Jesus was born.

Eventually, I knew it was time to leave Christianity and follow a different pathway to God.

Making the Move

This was not an easy decision; in fact, it was a spiritual struggle at the deepest level. Stephen Van Eck described it well when he wrote on the Deism.com website: "Once sucked into the parallel universe of Christianity, [a person] is too intimidated by threats and rationalizations to attempt escape. Even thinking along alternative lines will induce severe feelings of guilt."[2]

Of course, some would say my internal struggle was the result of "spiritual warfare" that was being waged between the spirit of God and Satan. I'll leave them to that belief. In actuality, it felt more like I was breaking free from a type of mind control.

Each step I took towards spiritual freedom was excruciating, but especially painful was the disapproval I faced from friends and family members who still believed in the Christian tradition. Any efforts to help them understand my decision were fruitless and often resulted in either an argument, a pleading to rethink my position, or simply a look of sympathy and concern. Nevertheless, I continued to press forward.

I want to stress that God remained a very important part of my life during this time. In fact, I often sought Him through meditation and prayer to overcome the anxiety and fear that rose up within me as I tried to break free from old beliefs. One that particularly haunted me was that I would be destined for the "lake of fire" if I didn't "believe in Jesus."

Was it all worth it? Absolutely! Once I opened my mental doorways and began thinking for myself instead of relying on the teachings of others, I began an exciting and rewarding spiritual journey that has resulted in a new, and much deeper, relationship with what I now call the "Universal Presence."

Time for Sharing

Throughout this process, I discovered there are many other Christians struggling with doubts and misgivings about their faith. Their anxiety and confusion compelled me to share what I have learned – and continue to learn – about the Christian faith. I believe readers will be amazed and surprised, as I was, that much of what they were taught in Sunday School has little basis in fact – or isn't addressed at all.

I want to emphasize that this book was not written to disparage Christian believers or to discount what they hold to be true in their heart. I wrote it because, as David Elkins said in the opening quote, so many of us live our lives simply accepting what others have told us.

To learn the truth about anything requires investigating the facts for yourself. It means opening your mind and allowing fresh information to enter. There is no doubt that examining new and/or different ideas and concepts about your faith can be scary. You may very well discover things that are in direct contrast with what you have always accepted as fact.

However, if your belief system induces fear and guilt at the deepest level of your being … if you have recurring doubts about any part of your Christian experience … if you are no longer willing to follow someone else's philosophy … if you are hungry for a deeper, more loving relationship with God, then you are ready to begin your own search for understanding.

As you embark upon this exciting journey, may you discover the God of love and acceptance. May you no longer be confused or confined by old beliefs. May you begin each day filled with anticipation and discovery, and may you end the day filled with gratitude in your heart. And most of all, may you find peace in your innermost being.

INTRODUCTION

I want to take you on a journey similar to the one I traveled in my search for understanding, so I begin with a history of the Bible. From there I move into a study of Jesus and Paul, the major players of Christianity. Then I present revealing information about a number of popular Christian beliefs. And finally, I share where my journey has taken me.

If you are a reader who likes to skip around rather than read each chapter in succession, here are brief descriptions to help you decide where to go next.

Chapter One discusses how and why the Bible was written, the role other cultures played in its creation, how it developed into the book it is today, whether it is truly without error, and much more.

Chapter Two focuses on Jesus, the center of Christian faith. However, in this chapter you may meet a Jesus unfamiliar to you. You probably believe he was sent by God to save the world from sin, but was this his true mission? Or did he have a different goal in mind?

Chapter Three covers the resurrection of Jesus and examines the events that occurred immediately afterwards. Can the empty tomb be considered proof that he returned to life? Who saw him? What did he look like?

Chapter Four questions the role of Paul in the establishment of the Christian church. Who was this man and why was his influence so great among early believers? Were his teachings the same as those of Jesus? Why was he called to evangelize the Gentiles?

Chapter Five examines Satan, the most feared entity in the Christian religion. Is it true that he was once an angel who rebelled against God and fell from heaven? Was he present in the

Garden of Eden? How did he evolve into a major player in the Christian religion?

Chapter Six reveals some facts about hell, also known as the "lake of fire." Is it a literal place? Are all non-believers destined to spend eternity there? Where did the concept of hell originate? Did the ancient Jews believe in hell?

Chapter Seven addresses the end times. Are we living in the "last days?" Did Jesus predict the end of the world? Did the author of Revelation really have a view of the future?

Chapter Eight centers on the dreaded figure known as the Antichrist. Is he alive today? Will he succeed in his sinister plan to take over the world? Will he face Jesus in a final battle between good and evil?

Chapter Nine presents the various views of God throughout the centuries, as well as how most people see God in today's world. In this final chapter, I also share how my concept of God has changed since leaving the Christian faith.

1. THE BIBLE: More Than Meets the Eye

"[T]ruth is so often, well ... not true."
—Carter Phipps, EnlightenNext Article

My search for understanding quite naturally began with the Bible, given that Christianity is rooted in the scriptures. In fact, as many scholars have observed, without the Bible there would be no Christianity since everything we know about Jesus is contained within its pages.

In his book, *Reading the Bible Again for the First Time*, Marcus Borg makes this observation: "How one sees the Bible and how one sees Christianity go hand in hand."[3] I think nearly all Christians see the Bible as a source of inspiration and guidance, but from there the perception changes by varying degrees.

Some see the Bible as the *literal* word of God and everything within its pages true and without error (infallible). Others see it as the *inspired* word of God and believe the Holy Spirit provided the precise ideas, thoughts, and concepts to the authors, who then wrote everything down in their own words using their own writing style.

Many more view the Bible as the *symbolic* word of God and believe it provides us with principles to live by through the use of stories and myths, metaphors and symbols.

An increasing number of scholars regard the Bible as a *historical* document. They search for its true meaning by examining the context of what each author writes, what is happening at that point in history, other writings from that time period, archeological evidence that supports or refutes what has been written, etc.

For the most part, a person's view of the Bible is shaped by early training, church doctrine, and/or personal bias. In my own case, I was influenced by the beliefs of the evangelical fundamentalist church I attended and saw the Bible as the Literal and Absolute Truth. (To see it as anything less was practically blasphemous!) Today, however, after extensive reading and research, I see the Bible from an entirely different perspective. I think one of the most astounding discoveries I made is how far Christian doctrine has strayed from its Hebrew roots.

From Whence Did It Come?

No matter how one regards the Bible, it has undeniably guided millions of people throughout the centuries. Yet, for all its influence, the history behind how it came to be remains unknown to a vast majority of believers. It was no different for me. I was taught it was "God's Word" and that was that. Not once was I encouraged to look into its beginnings.

Nevertheless, as I began my search for a deeper spiritual experience, I felt a driving desire to know more about its origin. Why was it written? Who were the people who wrote it? What were their beliefs? Is every word truly from God? How did it become the book it is today?

Shocking!

I was amazed and surprised at what I found out. In fact, the things I uncovered prompted a major shift in my belief system! Perhaps as you learn more about the sacred writings, you too will re-examine the "Good Book" and discover that things are not always as they seem.

New Or Used?

Long before the Bible was put into written form, the Hebrew people circulated stories about God by word of mouth, generation to generation, over thousands of years. We can be reasonably certain the accounts were modified and embellished over time because "memory is creatively reproductive rather than accurately recollective."[4] (An excellent example of this is illustrated in the old game of "Gossip," also known as "Telephone.")

While there is no question the Bible contains actual chronicles of the Hebrew people, scholars have traced the roots to many of the stories to ancient pagan myths circulating among early Babylonians, Sumerians, Phoenicians, Canaanites, and Egyptians -- all neighbors of the Israelites.

An oft-cited example is the "Epic of Gilgamesh,"[5] an epic poem from ancient Sumeria about the hero-king Gilgamesh of Uruk who ruled around 2500 BCE. This historical/mythological tale, said to be one of the oldest works of literature known to man, was originally written on 12 clay tablets in cuneiform script (an early ancient form of written expression).[6] Since the commonly accepted dates for the Pentateuch (the first five books of the Bible) are c. 1400-1200 BCE, this story preceded these writings by several thousand years.

In the "Epic," Gilgamesh is told of a "magic plant" called the "The Old Man Becomes a Young Man." This plant promises not only to make an old man young again, but also offers immortality to anyone who partakes of it. Gilgamesh is denied the opportunity of immortality because a "serpent" steals the plant while Gilgamesh is bathing.

It is not a large leap to discern a similarity to the story about Adam and Eve. In both stories mankind is denied immortality by a serpent – and it all relates to a plant or tree.

The "Epic" also includes a story about a flood remarkably similar to Noah's adventure. In both stories, humankind has angered God (the gods) because of sin and thus must be destroyed. Likewise, in both stories a warning of the coming disaster is given to someone seen as worthy of being spared during the destruction of mankind, and he is given specific instructions on how to save himself and his family. In the Bible,

Noah was instructed to: "Make thee an ark ..." and is given the exact measurements. In the Epic, Gilgamesh is instructed to "Tear down the house and build a boat" and he too is given exact measurements. Noah is instructed to bring "every living thing" into the boat; Gilgamesh is told to load his boat with "all living beings." At the end of the flood, both sent out birds (ravens and doves) to see if it was safe to disembark.

Borrowing ancient stories and beliefs from other cultures was not limited to writers of the Old Testament. There are numerous examples in the New Testament. Several of these are discussed in detail in later chapters.

The Written Word

Around 1000 BCE, the Hebrew alphabet was developed and Jewish scribes took on the task of putting these ancient tales in writing. There can be little doubt they injected their own perspectives, beliefs, desires, and understandings into what they wrote -- *and made alterations accordingly*. (Those who see the Bible as literal may be surprised to learn that even Jeremiah accused the scribes of writing falsely in Jeremiah 8:8.) It wasn't until after the Exile and the canonization of scripture that the scriveners became more conscientious about their efforts.

Writing these early manuscripts was laborious work; each story had to be copied word for word onto a papyrus or leather scroll. Once a manuscript became worn out, it was necessary to copy everything again. Certainly these early copyists were as careful as possible, but it is inevitable that some mistakes were made. Modern-day textual critics who compare ancient Bible manuscripts have found the entire meaning of a passage changed by a single stroke of the pen.[7]

In later years, trained monastery monks took over the job of copying texts, but this did not guarantee total accuracy. Below is an example of what scribes worked from. It is an excerpt from

Genesis 1 and illustrates what Bible text would have looked like if written in English prior to around 900 CE. It would have been in *scriptio continua* (continuous script), using only consonants and no vowels, capitalization, or punctuation, which is how early Hebrew was written.

Nthbgnnnggdcrtdthhvnndthrthndthrthwswthtfrmndvdnddrkn sswspnthfcfthdpndthsprtfgdmvdpnthfcfthwtrsndgdsdltthrblght ndthrwslghtndgdswthlghtthttwsgdndgddvddthlghtfrmthdrknss ndgdclldthlghtdndthdrknsshclldnghtndthvnngndthmrnngwrth frstdndgdsdltthrbfrmmntnthmdstfthwtrsndlttdvdthwtrsfrmthw trsndgdmdthfrmmntnddvddthwtrswhchwrndrthfrmmntfrmth wtrswhchwrbvthfrmmntndtwssndgdclldthfrmmnthvnndthvnn gndthmrnngwrthscnddndgdsdltthwtrsndrthhvnbgthrdtgthrnn plcndltthdrlndpprndtwssndgdclldthdrlndrthndthgthrngtgthrfth wtrsclldhssndgdswthttwsgdndgdsdltthrthbrngfrthgrssthhrbldng sdndthfrttrldngfrtftrhskndwhssdsntslfpnthrthndtwssndthrthbrg htfrthgrssndhrbldngsdftrhskndndthtrldngfrtwhssdw[8]

Now imagine you were a scribe responsible for precisely copying about 300 times this much text (the whole Bible), by hand, one character at a time. Can you be absolutely *sure* the entire copy would be free of even a single error?

While many Christians resist challenging the accuracy of Bible scripture, it is an accepted fact that human beings were doing the copying and humans are not infallible. Further, according to scholar Bart Ehrman,[9] many of the early scribes changed text because they thought it was *supposed* to be changed. If they saw what they felt to be a mistake or if a text disagreed with their own theological opinion, they altered it.

A Question of Authorship

The Bible includes writings by a number of authors – the traditional estimate is around forty. However, Bible scholars who study ancient manuscripts in great detail have discovered evidence that a number of books were authored by more than one person, thus increasing the overall total.

For example, it is generally accepted by many Jewish and Christian scholars that Moses wrote the first five books of the Bible – Genesis, Exodus, Leviticus, Numbers, and Deuteronomy. However, if you look closely at the text, you will notice a number of passages describing events that occurred *after* Moses' death, leaving no doubt that some unknown person took over as the writer.

Another example is the story of creation in Genesis. In Gen. 1:24-26, it says God created man *after* all the "living things," whereas in Gen 2:7-19, man was created *before* God made the "animals of the field." Moreover, in the first version, man and woman are created in a single act and in the second version, woman is created after (and from) man.

Further, God is called by two names in Genesis: *Yahweh* and *Elohim*, which has indicated to Bible scholars that two separate writers are involved, not only in the creation story but in several stories throughout the Pentateuch. Eventually, all accounts were blended together to form a continuous narrative.

Other indications that more than one person contributed to a Bible story are changes in tone or style within a single book, even the use of different words for the same object. This is reflected in the book of Isaiah and the gospel of Luke, among others

Mystery Authors

Another interesting fact about authorship is that although many books in the Bible are identified by name (Joshua, Samuel, Isaiah, Luke, Matthew, etc.), this does not mean the named individual was the author. It was not uncommon for lesser-known writers to attribute their writings to well-known figures of the time. As Paul Laughlin says, "some [are] named, some [are] claimed, and some [are] simply anonymous."[10]

This is particularly true of the canonical gospels. While many firmly believe they were written by the named apostles, in actuality there were numerous "gospels" being read and revered by the early Christians.[11] No one knew for sure who wrote what. It wasn't until sometime in the late second century that people began referring to the various writings by saying, "the gospel according to ..."

Putting It All Together

Not only were there countless gospels circulating after Jesus died, I learned there were also acts, epistles, and apocalypses[12] – each having very different perspectives from those that eventually became part of the New Testament. Some taught there were two gods – one of the Old Testament (the God of wrath) and one of the New Testament (a God of love and mercy). Not two different facets, but two different gods. Others maintained God did not create the world; it was the result of a cosmic disaster. Still others insisted Jesus was human only, others were certain he was completely divine, and some saw him as both. Ehrman[13] says the extensive theological diversity produced constant discussions, dialogues, and debates.

I also discovered during my research that there was a four hundred year span between the last writings of the Old Testament and the appearance of Jesus. Scholars refer to this time as the "intertestamental" (between the testaments) period, or the "silent" years. However, they were not really silent; people were still writing about God. Yet none of this written material is part of today's Bible. I wondered why.

The End Result

Jewish leaders canonized the 39 books of the Hebrew Bible (Old Testament) c. 250 BCE, but it was not until the end of the third century that agreement was finally reached about what would become the "official" books of the New Testament.

This task was taken up by a group of early church fathers who reviewed all existing manuscripts,[14] including the Apocryphal writings, to determine which should be "authorized" as sacred text and which should be ignored as heretical (most intertestamental writings[15]). As would be expected among human agents, there were a myriad of opinions with each person promoting his specific belief, agenda, and point of view.

Finally, the group came up with a set of criteria to assist their decision- making, including: was it written by an apostle, was it written in the first century, did it teach apostolic faith, did the writer claim inspiration. However, as one scholar points out, without the original manuscripts, there is no way of proving any of these criteria. Nonetheless, based on what they had, a vote was taken and a "canonized" version of the New Testament emerged, including the familiar four gospels.

But this is not the end of the story. Over the intervening years, additional councils formed and further discussions and debates were held. Some writings approved by the third century group were found to be heretical by later reviewers and were removed from the canon. Others were added. In fact, even today Bible scholars question whether particular books in the current Bible are sacred text. In addition, the Bible used by the Roman Catholic Church (and some eastern Christian churches) includes books that are rejected by Protestants.

Many Christians want to believe the Bible is the "inspired Word of God." However, how does one reconcile this belief with the knowledge that various individuals (humans) over the years have made different decisions about what was "inspired" scripture? Further, as one person remarked: "Why haven't there been any additional 'inspired by God writings' produced in the past 2,000 years? Did God go on strike?"

From Ancient to Modern

The Bible has been translated into more than 450 languages since its early beginnings. When considering the various translations of the Bible, it is important to recognize that "all translation is interpretation, and none is strictly literal."[16] In addition, it is not always possible to carry certain words or phrases in one language over to another while keeping their meaning or impact intact. An excellent example of this is the Hebrew word *almah*. In many versions of the Bible, the word is translated as "virgin" (a word with strong connotations in the English language). Jewish scholars declare this is incorrect because *almah* means "young woman" and denotes age, not virginity or sexual purity. The Hebrew word most commonly used for virgin is *bethulah*.

Along the Translation Pathway

The Old Testament was originally written in ancient Hebrew (Assyrian Script). During the Babylonian captivity as more and more of the Jewish community began speaking Aramaic,[17] Hebrew literacy declined. Thus, to help congregants during the reading of the Torah, the scriptures were translated into the common language.

Approximately 250 years later, the *lingua franca* of the Mediterranean area had become Greek so another translation of the Bible was produced. This translation, the *Septuagint* (LXX), was a work of many hands over many years. It contained what had become the 39 books of the Old Testament, along with the Apocrypha.[18] It was not in any way a literal translation of the

Hebrew Bible, but a highly interpretive one.[19] The early Christian writers used this translation when they quoted scripture.

In the late third century, Jerome, a Christian priest and apologist, was commissioned by Pope Damascus I to prepare a complete version of the Bible in Latin. Using the 39 books of the Septuagint, the 14 books of the Apocrypha, and the 27 books accepted as the New Testament (all written in Greek), he prepared what is known today as the *Vulgate* Bible.

It is an interesting side note that since the only organized and recognized church at that time in history was the Catholic Church, leadership refused to allow the Bible to be translated into any language *other* than Latin. In fact, it has been said that those in possession of non-Latin scriptures would be executed! However, this mattered little because most of the common people could not read Latin anyway and had to rely on the church for instruction.

The first English version of the Bible was produced in 1384 by John Wycliffe, who wanted to "put the Bible into the hands of the common people." This version, *handwritten* in Old English, was translated from the Vulgate Bible.

When the printing press was invented in 1456, the first published Bible was the Vulgate.

Between 1522 and 1534, Martin Luther translated the Bible into German. In a significant departure from the exclusive use of the Vulgate as a basis for translation, he used a Greek translation (produced in 1516 by *Erasmus*) for the New Testament and a Hebrew version (published in 1495) for the Old Testament.

In 1526, William Tyndale, using some of Luther's German translation, as well as earlier Greek versions, produced the first *printed* version of the New Testament in English.

Between the years of 1526 and 1593, the Bible was translated into Dutch, French, Spanish, and Czech.

In 1604, King James I authorized the translation that came to bear his name. It was finally published in 1611 and contained all 80 books (the Apocrypha was officially removed in 1885, leaving only 66 books). This translation remains the most widely circulated Bible in existence today and thousands of Christians believe it to be the only "authentic" version of the Bible. In fact, some have even been known to become quite upset when newer translations are mentioned. An example of this is a story about a woman who made the following comment when her pastor said he wanted to introduce a more recent translation to the congregation: "In my opinion, if the King James Version was good enough for Jesus, it's good enough for us!"

And There's More

The preceding is a condensed list of dates and times when the Bible was restated from one language to another. There are many, many others, plus there are numerous "versions" in circulation (e.g., Authorized Standard, New International, New American Standard, New King James, Revised Standard), all derived from the "Authorized" (King James) Bible but which use updated and/or contemporary language. Other versions have been translated to reinforce particular doctrinal beliefs.

Timing Is Everything

For years, I saw the Bible as one long story and assumed the stories occurred in chronological order. I admit I was somewhat taken aback to discover this is not the case. As a result, it changed my understanding about what really happened throughout both Jewish and Christian history.

While it is impossible to know the exact dates when each book was written, Bible scholars can pinpoint approximate dates based on several factors, including secular history and archeological finds (see Appendix). One example I came across is the book of Isaiah. I learned it was written anywhere between 50-100 years *before* First and Second Kings -- yet its placement in the Bible is ten books later. In the New Testament, an astounding fact is that Paul's letters *predate* the gospels. Paul's first writings are dated around 50-60 CE while the earliest gospel (Mark) was not created until around 65 CE. John's gospel was not written until c. 90-120 CE! This means the theories of Paul (see Chapter Four) were already in circulation several years before the gospel writers and, undoubtedly, colored their view of Jesus' words and activities.

God's Word?

As previously mentioned, some Christians contend the Bible is infallible; that is, completely true and without error. They believe everything within its pages was directly imbued into the thoughts and minds of the writers by none other than God. For many others, this is a difficult concept to swallow, especially when considering scriptures such as those listed below:

How many animals did Noah collect?

Genesis 7:2-3 – *Take with you seven pairs of all clean animals, the male and its mate; and a pair of the animals that are not clean, the male and its mate; and seven pairs of the birds of the air also, male and female*

Genesis 7:15 – *They went into the ark with Noah, two and two of all flesh in which there was the breath of life.*

Who built the ark of the covenant?

Deuteronomy 10:3 – *So I [Moses] made an ark of acacia wood*

Exodus 37:1 – *Bezalel made the ark of acacia wood*

Who killed Goliath?

1 Samuel 17:50 – *So David prevailed over the Philistine [Goliath] with a sling and a stone, striking down the Philistine and killing him*

2 Samuel 21:19 – *...Elhanan son of Jaare-oregim, the Bethlehemite, killed Goliath the Gittite*

What happened to Judas?

Matthew 27:5 – *Throwing down the pieces of silver in the temple, he departed; and he went and hanged himself.*

Acts 1:18 – *Now this man acquired a field with the reward of his wickedness; and falling headlong, he burst open in the middle and all his bowels gushed out.*

Paul's vision

Acts 9:7 – *The men who were traveling with him stood speechless because they heard the voice but saw no one.*

Acts 22:9 – *Now those who were with me saw the light but did not hear the voice*

Which version is correct? How do we choose? What criteria do we use?

There are also two descriptions in the Bible of the Abrahamic covenant, two stories of the naming of Isaac, two accounts of God changing Jacob's name to Israel, plus several other "doublets." In a few cases, triplets have been found; that is, the same account appears three times.[20]

Some theologians say the *original* scriptures were perfect and without error but through copy errors and translation this perfection was lost. Since there are no original manuscripts in existence, a statement like this is speculative at best.

Rather than looking at the Bible as a "literal road map to reality," I agree with Spong's assessment that it is more of a "historic narrative of the journey our religious forebears made in the eternal human quest to understand life, the world, themselves, and God."[21]

Final Thoughts

Probably one of the most important things to remember about the Bible is that the authors were writing about the cultures, events, and people of their time. They were telling us "how *they* saw things, not about how *God* sees things."[22] They were describing *their* experiences, *their* beliefs, *their* views about the world in which they lived.

Moreover, it was common among early writers to write with a story-telling bias, putting words into the mouths of principals to make it more interesting ... *and* to reinforce what they wanted to get across by referencing an important person. As Wylen notes, writers were "expected to have the literary skill to place stirring and appropriate speeches in the mouths of the chief characters at significant moments."[23]

To truly understand the Bible, it needs to be read through the lens of the cultures for which it was originally written. Trying to project back into its pages later developments and/or interpretations frequently misconstrues the meaning and message the authors sought to convey. Further, Bible readers of today live in circumstances that could not have been imagined by the original writers.

Even so, one cannot deny that the Bible is filled with words of wisdom about life and living. Many individual scriptures offer guidance, comfort, and even an occasional chastening. But to read the Bible as a literal chronicle of events is to take away from its primary purpose.

Essentially, the Bible is a *human* product generated in response to God. To accept this premise does not deny the reality of God; it simply helps us to understand "the sacred is known not in a set of statements about God, but experientially, as a mystery beyond all language."[24]

2. JESUS: Messiah? Savior? God?

"God is not somewhere else, but right here and everywhere."
– Marcus J. Borg[25]

During my years within Christianity, my vision of Jesus was no different than thousands of other Christians. He was the Savior of the World, Son of God, Christ, Messiah, King of Kings, Lamb of God, the Word, Bread of Life, Redeemer, and second member of the Trinity.

I completely accepted the stories about his death and resurrection. I fully believed that only through him would I find salvation and favor with God. I eagerly anticipated his glorious return when he would set up the kingdom of God on a newly-created earth.

After I embarked upon my search for understanding, I began to see Jesus in a new light. I learned that he did not come to save lost souls and get them into heaven. He did not see himself as the "Son of Man"[26] who planned to return to earth at some future time to set up the kingdom of God. He did not profess to be the Messiah. And he never claimed to be divine.

I struggled with this new information. It was in direct contrast to what I had always been taught. To view Jesus in this way meant putting aside strongly held beliefs and filtering out the teachings that had been a part of my life for many years.

Yet, little by little, as I opened my heart and mind to new ideas and possibilities, a different Jesus began to emerge. Rather than coming to die for the sins of the world, I realized this humble man of Galilee came to deliver a message to the Jewish people – a message that he believed would revolutionize their concept of God. Unfortunately, after his death certain individuals re-interpreted what he said, bestowed upon him the title "Son of God," and transformed him into an object of worship. In later years, it was decreed he was God incarnate.

It took a long while to dig out from under years of church dogma, but eventually I came to understand what this remarkable man came to accomplish. As you read the following pages, perhaps you too will gain a new perspective of this man who influenced so many.

The Jesus of the Bible

For over two thousand years, Christians have seen Jesus through the eyes of the gospel writers, believing they were disciples of Jesus and eyewitnesses to the events they described. Many may be surprised, as I was, to learn this is not the case.

Nearly all modern biblical scholars agree the gospels were written *several decades*[27] after Jesus' death by *unknown* authors,[28] none of which knew Jesus personally or were present at any of the events they described. Not only is this evidenced by the number of discrepancies in the various accounts, but even the author of Luke writes the information he recorded was "handed on" to him (Luke 1:2).

Furthermore, following tradition, the writers did not write historical facts; they wrote *stories* about Jesus[29] – much as a fiction author would do today – based on hearsay that spread after his death. They even copied content from other manuscripts that were in circulation.[30] In other words, the gospels were created from *received* information, filtered and modified by imaginative writers.

According to E.P. Sanders[31] and others, the goal was not to provide a biography of Jesus, but rather to express and reinforce a faith-based perspective of this man who walked the dusty roads of Palestine. As C.H. Dodd puts it, each gospel was "a report of certain happenings, together with, and inseparably interwoven with, an interpretation of these happenings."[32] Yet centuries of

Christians have taken these accounts at face value and experienced little difficulty in explaining away inconsistencies.

I soon realized if I truly wanted to know who Jesus was, I had to look beyond what is written in the gospels, remove the garments of religious belief, and explore the world in which he lived.

A Different Perspective

Something I had not taken into account in my vision of *Yeshua* (Hebrew for Jesus) was that he was deeply Jewish. Not only was he Jewish by birth, but he practiced Jewish customs and taught Jewish doctrines in Jewish synagogues. His followers were Jews and he was looked upon as a Jewish leader (according to the gospels, some even called him a rabbi[33]).

Many saw him as a great teacher and healer. The first century historian, Flavius Josephus, characterized him as a "wise man" and a "performer of astonishing deeds."[34]

As I considered this view of Jesus, a new image began to form. It did not diminish his place in history, but it altered my beliefs about who he was and why he left such an impact on the people of the first century.

The World Prior To Jesus

I began to explore the world in which the Jewish people lived before Jesus. I discovered that events of the previous centuries had turned their world upside down. They were confused and bewildered at what was happening and were desperate for a message from God.

An Arduous Journey

For most of their history, the Jewish people had seen *Yahweh* (YHWH) as a god who intervened on their behalf through such events as the Exodus, the conquest of Palestine, and the establishment of the Davidic kingdom. They saw him as a Divine Leader who appointed rulers, toppled enemies, and passed historical judgment on their good and bad actions.[35] Through it all, they looked to the day when *Yahweh* would fulfill his promise to Abraham and establish Israel as a great nation under a peaceful theocracy.

However, after King Nebuchadnezzar conquered the land of Judah in 587 BCE, destroyed the city of Jerusalem and Solomon's temple, and exiled the people to Babylon, things began to change. Now they were forced to live as foreigners in a strange land, they could no longer worship and perform sacrificial rites, and little by little they saw their cultural identity fading away.

Then in 532 BCE, the Persians conquered Babylon and the new ruler, Cyrus the Great, gave the Jews permission to return to Judah, their home country, and rebuild their temple. Many, but not all, of the people took advantage of this offer and a new temple was constructed under the guidance of Ezra and Nehemiah. Although still under Persian rule, priests were allowed to become the political and religious leaders of these satellite Jewish communities.

The Jewish emigrants were overjoyed. They had reclaimed their country, rebuilt the temple, and restored worship. Unfortunately, their joy was short-lived. A terrible drought occurred and the Judean farmers struggled to make a living. On top of that, a horde of locusts descended and destroyed much of the crops. Wylen, a rabbi who studies Jewish history, writes of widespread doubt about the existence of God during this time.[36]

Adding to their despair, they stopped receiving messages from God through their prophets (individuals chosen to speak on God's behalf to the people and convey a message or teaching). They could not understand why God had become so distant.

Alexander Stakes His Claim

Around 330 BCE, Alexander the Great swept through the Mediterranean area with his military forces and overcame the Persian Empire, which included the land of Judah. This was not simply a military or political victory; Alexander's presence profoundly influenced the spiritual life of the Jewish people. As an ardent student of Greek philosophy, he required Greek thought and culture to be promoted in every land he conquered. The Persian-based Jews, who were more profoundly influenced by these new ideas than their Judean counterparts, eventually became known as the Hellenistic Jews. It was the Hellenistic Jews who were principally responsible for the spread of Christianity in the first century CE.

Alexander died in 323 BCE and two of his top generals, Ptolemy and Seleucus, divided his empire into two kingdoms – Egypt and Syria-Mesopotamia. Judah was on the border between the two kingdoms and initially fell under Ptolemy, who ruled Egypt. After approximately one hundred years, the Seleucids, who were more powerful than the Egyptians, pushed aside the Ptolemies and took over both kingdoms.

Even with all the transitions, Wylen reports that overall, Jewish society remained relatively stable throughout the centuries of Persian, Ptolemaic, and Seleucid rule.[37] The Judean high priests were allowed to continue teaching the Torah and perform the traditional rites and sacrifices under both monarchies; however, Greek ideas and practices continued to infiltrate and influence the people.

A Crushing Blow

Then in 175 BCE, a terrible event shook the Jewish people and their religion to its very foundation.

The tyrannical Seleucid King Antiochus IV became ruler and immediately began persecuting the Jewish people. He eliminated the high priesthood, outlawed the Torah, forbad ritual sacrifice, and set up an altar in the Jewish temple dedicated to the Greek god, Zeus. He forced the people, under threat of execution, not only to worship this god but also to eat pork (a forbidden food) sacrificed in its honor. As a result, by default, Hellenism became the dominant way of life throughout the entire Jewish community.

Messages from God

During this time of revolution and change, scores of writers arose, each declaring to have "messages from God," revealed to them through dreams and visions. Whereas ancient Jewish prophets wrote of current times and events and included promises of the temporal restoration of the nation under a future Davidic king, these apocalyptic[38] writers took a different tack.

In an attempt to explain why God's people suffered at the hands of ungodly rulers and why the establishment of the promised kingdom had yet to manifest, they wrote of a future day when God would dramatically intervene to destroy evil and bring an end to the people's troubles. In these messages, they "spun out fanciful predictions of the coming end of the world and dramatic descriptions of the aftermath."[39] Nearly all proclaimed the world would end in a cosmic cataclysm, followed by a "new heaven and new earth."

Prior to the exile, Hebrew writings did not mention anything about the world ending. So where did these radical ideas come from? They came from *Zoroastrianism*, the dominant religion of the Persians, among whom the Jewish people had lived for approximately two centuries.

Zoro Who?

Before beginning my research, I had never heard of the Zoroastrian religion. I was surprised to learn it is considered to be the oldest of the revealed world religions,[40] although its origins are shrouded in mystery. Scholars generally agree it was founded by the Iranian prophet and reformer Zoroaster in the 6th century BCE.[41] (Tradition holds that Judaism dates back to c. 1200-1400 BCE.) Today, there are around two hundred thousand adherents of Zoroastrianism, most of whom live in India and modern day Iran.

I was especially fascinated by the similarity in Zoroastrian beliefs and what I had been taught as a Christian. One of their main beliefs is that there is one all-wise, wholly just and good, creator God (*Ahura Mazda*), who is in charge of all the good that happens in the world. Opposing *Ahura Mazda* is an evil spirit, *Angra Mainyu*, who is responsible for all the world's evils. There is an ongoing cosmic struggle between these two beings and sometime in the future, a final spiritual battle will take place with Evil defeated. The world is then purged and a new world is created with *Ahura Mazda* reigning supreme.[42]

None of these beliefs were part of ancient Judaism,[43] but as the Jewish people endured the hardships of living under foreign rule, the stories spun by the apocalyptic writers, who drew heavily from Zoroastrianism, had great appeal. Attributing their hardships to some evil force allowed them to maintain the belief that *Yahweh* still cared and would one day destroy their enemies once and for all. The seed of dualism had been planted and it didn't take long until the concept of "Satan" began to fully develop (see Chapter 5).

There were other Zoroastrian concepts that infiltrated the Jewish belief system, including the existence of angels and demons (who assist the forces of Good and Evil), future resurrection of the body, the concept of heaven and hell, and a final judgment with rewards and punishment. A particularly relevant belief to the later Christian movement was that in the end, a great savior (*Saoshyant*), born of a virgin, will restore all goodness.

Enter Jesus

Now we have an idea of the world into which Jesus was born. The people had come to believe in angels and demons, an evil force in opposition to *Yahweh*, and a future cosmic upheaval. Death was no longer a shadowy existence in *sheol*,[44] but was now seen as a stopping place until the day of judgment when either reward or punishment would be meted out for earthly deeds.

Yet, while many of the old teachings had been replaced with new ones, the people never lost sight of their one great hope – that the divinely appointed Messiah foretold by the prophet Isaiah would one day appear, remove oppression and injustice, and usher in the glorious reign of God. For some, *Yeshua* seemed to be that person.

Who Was Jesus and Why Did He Come?

Although taught that Jesus came to offer himself as a sacrifice to God for the sins of the world, the more I read and studied, the more convinced I became that this was *not* his true mission. Instead, historical evidence supports he came as a *prophet*[45] to share a message from God with the Jewish people. It wasn't until after his death that the message, and its recipients, changed (see Chapter 4).

It is unclear how early Jesus was aware of his mission. From the Bible stories, this revelation seems to have taken place when he encountered John the Baptist.

The Role of John the Baptist

John was a popular Jewish apocalyptic preacher who proclaimed that God, very soon, in the near future, intended to eradicate the evil of the world in a fiery judgment. He warned his listeners that they needed to get right with God, repent of their sins, follow the way of the Lord by showing mercy and justice to others, and remove all impurity by immersing themselves in the *mikvah* – a body of living water (in this case, the Jordan River). This cleansing ritual was a requirement for any Jew that visited the temple so they recognized its importance as a sign of penitence.[46]

Imagine Jesus walking along the banks of the Jordan River one sunny afternoon. He sees the crowd of people and hears John shouting his message of the coming kingdom. He listens for a while and then he too submits to John's baptism. As he emerges from the cool waters, he has an epiphany and becomes acutely aware of God's calling upon his life. The Bible tells us he immediately retreats to the wilderness, probably to think things over and decide his course of action. After forty days (Mark 1:13) he emerges from the wilderness, confident of his mission:

I must proclaim the good news of the kingdom of God ... for I was sent for this purpose. (Luke 4:43)

What was the "good news" Jesus came to proclaim? Christians see it as being related to God's plan for salvation. However, I believe it was about the establishment of a new relationship between God and the Jewish people. Jesus wanted to let them know the barriers between them and *Yahweh* had been forever removed.

Jesus' Message

John the Baptist preached about God's *impending* reign,[47] but Jesus saw things much differently. In his eyes, the kingdom was *already present*. It did not exist in some far-off reality; it was here ... *now*. In Mark, he said it is *at hand*; in Matthew, he declared it *has come upon you*; and in Luke, he told the people it is *within you*.

Jesus wanted his people to know there was no need to wait for *Yahweh's* presence to manifest because God was all around them and within them. Over and over, through parable and deed, he declared that God was with each person at this moment ... in this instant.

He regularly manifested *Yahweh's* inner presence through his demonstrations of love and concern for others – and he urged his followers to do the same. He encouraged them to be forgiving of one another, to show kindness and compassion, to love their enemies, to bless those that cursed them, and to do good to those that hated them. His most profound directive was when he told them (and us) to "love your neighbor as yourself." (Matthew 22:39)

How Can This Be?

The idea of an immediate and indwelling kingdom was a difficult, if not impossible, concept for the Jews to accept. It had been a long-standing belief that God resided in the "upper heavens" – accessible only through the priests, the law, and sacrifices. Even though Jesus repeatedly tried to explain that God's kingdom could not be seen, that it was not "here" or "there," (Luke 17:20-21) the people were unable to comprehend how God could be a personal and immediate presence in their lives.

Moreover, throughout the past several centuries, they had been told by the apocalyptic writers that the establishment of God's reign would take place sometime in the *future* and be preceded by supernatural events in the heavens. Further, they believed it would be a *physical* kingdom ruled by the *mashiach* (the "anointed one"), a great political leader descended from King David. (Jeremiah 23:5)

As a result, they (as well as Christians today) dismissed Jesus' message and continued to wait for a future kingdom, one that would manifest only after evil is destroyed and the wicked punished; a *physical* kingdom existing in a restored earth where the faithful would be with God forever.

Final Thoughts

From a strictly historical viewpoint, unless ancient texts come to light, we will never know exactly who Jesus was. But as scholars have researched and gathered information about him over the years, it becomes more and more evident his primary mission was to deliver a special message from God to the Jewish people.

He wanted them to know that God's kingdom was present *now*, not in some nebulous future. There was no need to wait for some cosmic cataclysm, nor was there any ritual, law, or sacrifice to fulfill. God's love and mercy were immediately accessible.

As I considered this new perspective of Jesus, I thought of something he reportedly told his listeners: "I came that they may have life, and have it abundantly" (John 10:10). To me, he was saying we should enjoy the richness of life in the here and now. There is no need to wait for some future event to occur. We can be in God's presence at this very moment.

I believe this is the "good news of the kingdom" that Jesus came to proclaim.

3. JESUS: Second Time Around

"If there is no resurrection of the dead, then Christ has not been raised; and if Christ has not been raised, then our proclamation has been in vain and your faith has been in vain" (1 Corinthians 15:13-14)

For years, I accepted the Christian doctrine that Jesus died as a sacrifice for the sins of humankind, was resurrected from the dead, ascended to heaven, and is now sitting at the right hand of God. Although the whole scenario stretches the rational mind, I never questioned what I was told. I simply believed.

It wasn't until I was deep into my search for understanding that I realized I had never fully read the scriptures related to the resurrection and later appearances of Jesus. Certainly I knew all about the Easter story and was *familiar* with what was written in the gospels, but I had never done a thorough read. Once I did, I was amazed at what I found.

To illustrate what I discovered, I'm presenting the scriptural texts related to the resurrection story below. They are presented in the order in which Bible historians have determined they were written.

The Resurrection According To:
Mark 16:1-8

When the Sabbath was over, Mary Magdalene, and Mary the mother of James, and Salome bought spices, so that they might go and anoint him. And very early on the first day of the week, when the sun had risen, they went to the tomb. They had been saying to one another, "Who will roll away the stone for us from the entrance to the tomb?" When they looked up, they saw that the stone, which was very large, had already been rolled back. As they entered the tomb, they saw a young man, dressed in a white robe, sitting on the right side; and they were alarmed.

But he said to them, "Do not be alarmed: you are looking for Jesus of Nazareth, who was crucified. He has been raised; he is not here. Look, there is the place they laid him. But go, tell his disciples and Peter that he is going ahead of you to Galilee; there you will see him, just as he told you." So they went out and fled from the tomb, for terror and amazement had seized them; and they said nothing to anyone, for they were afraid.[48]

Matthew 28:1-8

After the Sabbath, as the first day of the week was dawning, Mary Magdalene and the other Mary went to see the tomb. And suddenly there was a great earthquake; for an angel of the Lord, descending from heaven, came and rolled back the stone and sat on it. His appearance was like lightning and his clothing white as snow. For fear of him the guards shook and became like dead men. But the angel said to the women, "Do not be afraid; I know that you are looking for Jesus who was crucified. He is not here; for he has been raised, as he said. Come, see the place where he lay. Then go quickly and tell his disciples. He has been raised from the dead, and indeed he is going ahead of you to Galilee; there you will see him. This is my message for you." So they left the tomb quickly with fear and great joy, and ran to tell his disciples.

Luke 24:1-10

But on the first day of the week, at early dawn, they came to the tomb, taking the spices that they had prepared. They found the stone rolled away from the tomb, but when they went in, they did not find the body. While they were perplexed about this, suddenly two men in dazzling clothes stood beside them. The women were terrified and bowed their faces to the ground, but the men said to them, "Why do you look for the living among the dead? He is not here, but has risen. Remember how he told you, while he was still in Galilee, that the Son of Man must be handed over to sinners, and be crucified, and on the third day rise again." Then they remembered his words, and returning from the tomb, they told all this to the eleven and to all the rest. Now it was Mary Magdalene, Joanna, Mary the mother of James, and the other women with them who told this to the apostles.

John 20:1-13

Early on the first day of the week, while it was still dark, Mary Magdalene came to the tomb and saw that the stone had been removed from the tomb. So she ran and went to Simon Peter and the other disciple, the one whom Jesus loved, and said to them, "They have taken the Lord out of the tomb, and we do not know where they have laid him." Then Peter and the other disciple set out and went toward the tomb. The two were running together, but the other disciple outran Peter and reached the tomb first. He bent down to look in and saw the linen wrappings lying there, but he did not go in. Then Simon Peter came, following him, and went into the tomb. He saw the linen wrappings lying there, and the cloth that had been on Jesus' head, not lying with the linen wrappings but rolled up in a place by itself. Then the other disciple, who reached the tomb first, also went in and he saw and believed; for as yet they did not understand the scripture, that he must rise from the dead. Then the disciples returned to their homes.

But Mary stood weeping outside the tomb. As she wept, she bent over to look into the tomb; and she saw two angels in white, sitting where the body of Jesus had been lying, one at the head and the other at the feet. They said to her, "Woman, why are you weeping?" She said to them, "They have taken away my Lord and I do not know where they have laid him."

What's the Real Scoop?

Like many other believers, I had a vision of what took place on that eventful morning. Several women visited and found an empty tomb. There was an earthquake. An angel appeared and said Jesus had risen. The guards became like dead men. The women were told to go and tell the disciples what they had witnessed.

But is this what really happened? Upon closer examination, I was surprised to find the gospel writers each had a slightly different version. In fact, they agreed on only three things: (1) Mary Magdalene visited the tomb, (2) it was on the first day of the week, and (3) the tomb was empty.

They did not agree on: the precise time the women visited the tomb; the number and identity of the women; the purpose of their visit; the appearance of the messenger(s) – angelic or human; what the women were told; the women's response.

How do we account for these variations? Considering that none of the gospel writers were eyewitnesses, plus the fact the gospels were written *several decades* after the death of Jesus, it is highly likely the resurrection accounts were based on oral tradition. In fact, as previously noted, the writer of Luke commented at the beginning of his gospel that he was writing about things that had been "handed on" to him.

Many feel the noted differences are unimportant. They point to the theme that runs throughout each story – Jesus was not in the tomb. For them, the words written over two thousand years ago about a dead man missing from a grave is all they need to affirm their belief in the resurrection.

Jesus Died

From a rational perspective, all we know for certain is that Jesus died. However, for millions of people the story doesn't end there.

What is Death?

Death is defined as the complete and permanent cessation of all vital bodily functions (circulatory, respiratory, and brain). Within hours after death, rigor mortis sets in and various degenerative processes begin. There have been no reliable or scientific reports of anyone regaining their vital functions once they have totally ceased. Although there are various medical interventions in our modern-day society that can delay death, no such devices or methods existed in the first century. Conclusion: death is final and irreversible.[49]

But Where's the Body?

If, as the gospel writers report, the tomb was empty – where did the body go? Did Jesus actually get up and walk away as Christians believe? Was his body stolen? Or was the body missing for some other reason?

Several theories have been advanced over the years about what might have happened to Jesus' body (some of them pretty far-fetched), but since no one was *actually present* when the body left the tomb, it's all speculation. Until some type of archeological evidence turns up, the disposal of the body must remain unknown.

The Matter of Resurrection

The concept of death is not clearly defined in the ancient Hebrew teachings, primarily because the Jewish people were more interested in present life than afterlife.[50] If it was considered at all, it was believed the dead went to *sheol*, a place of shadowy nothingness where the good and the bad slept for eternity. According to Jewish scholar Stephen Wylen, there was no reward or punishment after death.[51]

It wasn't until the Babylonian exile and, subsequently, the Persian takeover that the Jews began to change their views on what happens at death. By the time of Jesus, the Zoroastrian belief that the dead would be resurrected had permeated the Jewish communities and nearly every Jew anticipated some sort of afterlife. Once we realize this was the common mindset, it is not difficult to see why the resurrection story spread – and why it was believed.

Now You See Him ...

According to the Bible, Jesus made several after-death appearances; however, the circumstances surrounding these appearances are somewhat puzzling. On three occasions, he is not immediately recognizable (why not?). On two other occasions, he suddenly appears in the middle of a locked room. To some of his disciples, he seems to be a ghost. Another observer sees him as a "light from heaven."

The writer of John's gospel tells us that one of the disciples (Thomas) touched Jesus' body, and Luke's author reports that he ate and drank with the disciples. In Matthew's gospel, it says that two of the women saw him as they were leaving the empty tomb and touched his feet. John reports that Mary tried to cling ("hold on") to him. Each of these occurrences would indicate Jesus had a physical body, yet Paul maintains he returned to life with a *spiritual* body (1 Corinthians 15:44). Why, and how, did the story get changed?

Luke's gospel reports that Jesus was around after death for only a few hours; in John's gospel, he was seen up to a week after his death; and the writer of Acts says he was present for 40 days.

One gospel account says Jesus was seen by the "eleven" (Judas was no longer alive), while Paul says he appeared to "the twelve." Paul also reports Jesus was seen by Cephas, 500 brothers and sisters, James, and all the apostles (1 Corinthians 15:5-7). Interestingly, Paul (whose writings predate the gospels) says nothing about an empty tomb or Jesus' appearance to the women mentioned in the gospel stories.

A fact many people often overlook is that the resuscitated Jesus appeared almost exclusively to his followers. Paul is the only exception and even then, Jesus did not appear in physical form but as a "light from heaven." Many scholars wonder why he limited his appearances. Why didn't he appear to all the people?

Outside of the gospels, there is no mention of a man named Jesus returning to life. Not one word. One would certainly think that reports of a formerly dead man walking around and talking to various people (at one point, 500 at a time) would have been considered a miraculous event and be recorded by other writers living at the time.

Now You Don't

The stories about Jesus returning to life and appearing to various individuals undoubtedly caused quite a stir. The people were buzzing among themselves, asking one another if they had seen him. Then, after a period of time, all the hearsay seemed to die down. There were no more reported sightings and the people started asking, "Where is he now?" Someone answers, "I don't know. He seems to have disappeared." Then one of Jesus' followers chimes in, "He's not here anymore because he's been carried up into heaven" (Luke 24:51).

An important fact to keep in mind is how the people of the first century viewed earth. To them, it was circular and more or less flat, much like a dinner plate. Around the edge, there were columns of mountains that held up a rigid firmament (the sky). This firmament was believed to be relatively close to the earth – a few thousand feet or so in the air. Along the underside of the firmament were angels, who were responsible for pushing the sun, moon, planets and stars along during the day and night.

Above this firmament was Heaven – and this is where they believed God lived.

It all made perfect sense. Jesus had gone to be with God …who dwelled above the sky. Not only that, in the Hellenistic world (of which the Jews were a part), it was commonplace for great heroes to be taken up to dwell among the gods as a reward for a life well lived.

What I find somewhat incredible is that Christians today, who have known for years that earth is a planet located in a galaxy within a vast universe, still believe in a God that is somewhere "up there … above the sky."

As with the resurrection, outside of the Bible there are no verifiable accounts of Jesus (or anyone else, for that matter) physically leaving this earth and ascending into the heavens.

Third Time Around?

To this day, many in the Christian world believe Jesus is seated at the right hand of God and will one day return on the clouds of heaven (Matthew 26:64) to set up a kingdom of peace and love. Certainly if such an unprecedented event were to take place, it would authenticate the biblical story that a man named Jesus lived, died, and returned to life. However, until that time and without verifiable evidence that a resurrection ever took place, such a belief simply doesn't hold water.

Final Thoughts

The Christian religion essentially hangs on the scripture presented at the beginning of this chapter – if there is no resurrection, then faith in Jesus and his role as savior serves no purpose. In other words, Christianity stands or falls on the merits of the Easter story.

Is the story true? We will never know because the resurrection "evidence" is all based on Bible scripture. There is no historical or scientific proof that such a "miracle" ever took place and, like creation, there were no witnesses.

What we do know is that the people of Jesus' time believed in supernatural events. They had been exposed to the stories about Moses and the Red Sea, Joshua and the battle of Jericho, Jonah and the whale, among others. Add to that the belief in resurrection of the dead inherited from the Zoroastrians and it is easy to understand why they thought Jesus had returned to life.

Putting aside the story of the resurrection and looking at Jesus from a strictly rational viewpoint, there is little argument that during his lifetime he brought to the Jewish people (and subsequently, to the rest of the world) a profound spiritual truth about the nature of God. He was an extraordinary man who truly cared about people and wanted them to know that God's love is accessible to everyone – with no strings attached.

Unfortunately, over time, the message Jesus delivered has been significantly altered and access to God has become encumbered by human-imposed rules and regulations.

4. PAUL: A Man With a Mission

"Paul's words are not the Words of God. They are the words of Paul – a vast difference."
– John Shelby Spong[52]

Throughout my Christian experience, I viewed Paul (first called Saul) as the model Christian. I held him in high esteem and strived to follow his teachings. Through his writings, I gained inspiration and instructions on how to live. He encouraged me to love, to remain faithful, to not get discouraged when things were tough, and most of all, he gave me hope for a blessed future with Christ.

However, as I delved into the history of Paul, I soon realized this icon of the faith was not who I thought he was. I discovered that many of the doctrines he taught were not from Jesus; they were from Paul. He had fashioned a religion *about* Jesus, not *of* Jesus. And everything he taught started with a mystical visitation he received on the Road to Damascus.

The Visitation

"Those crazy Jesus people! Claiming their leader got up and walked away from his tomb. They're out of their minds! Nobody dies and then comes back to life. Not only that, they're causing all sorts of ruckus in the community with their ideas that this guy was the Messiah and he's going to return to earth and set up God's kingdom. They need to be put away before their ideas spread any further!"

These were very possibly the thoughts that were swirling around in Paul's head as he walked along the road to Damascus, authorization in hand from the Judean High Priest to arrest anyone (man or woman) who followed "The Way" and bring them to Jerusalem (Acts 9:1-2) where they would be punished and put into prison.

We can almost feel his anticipation – walking as fast as he could on the rough and rocky road, visions in his head of grabbing the infidels, wrapping their ankles in chains, and forcing them to recant their claims about this man Jesus – when suddenly, something very strange happens. A "light from heaven" flashes all around him.

The eerie brilliance startles him so much that Paul immediately falls to the ground. As he's lying there in the dirt, he hears a voice calling his name, but sees nothing.

"Saul, Saul, why are you persecuting me?"

"What? What do you mean? Who is this?" Paul asks.

The voice replies, "I am Jesus, whom you are persecuting. Now get up and continue your journey to Damascus where you will be told what to do" (Acts 9:3-6).

As Paul struggles to his feet, disoriented and confused, he realizes he's unable to see. He reaches out for help from the soldiers that are accompanying him, and the small band continues its journey to Damascus.

Meanwhile, as the story goes, Jesus ("the Lord") also reveals himself in a vision to a man named Ananias, a devout and highly respected Jew who lives in Damascus. Ananias is told to find Paul, heal his blindness, convince him that what he experienced was a divine manifestation, and then instruct him to share what he has seen and heard with the Gentiles (Acts 9:10-12).

But what has Paul seen and heard – a blinding light and a phantom voice?

If You Don't Get It Right The First Time ...

I then discovered there are three different versions in the Book of Acts (9:3-19, 22:6-21, 26:12-18) of Paul's otherworldly experience (amazing how I never noticed this before) – and it isn't until the *final* version that we actually learn the message delivered to Paul.

In that final account, it is approximately 58 CE (some 20 years after Jesus' mysterious visitation) and it seems Paul has spent the last two years in prison at Caesarea for spreading his message of "salvation by Jesus." King Agrippa and his wife come to visit the area and Paul asks for, and is granted, an opportunity to plead his case before the king. After providing a brief history of his life up to this point, as well as a description of his Damascus Road experience, we finally learn what "the voice" told him – that he is to go to the Gentiles to "open their eyes so that they may turn from darkness to light, and from the power of Satan[53] to God, so that they may receive forgiveness of sins ..." (Acts 26:18).

This is the only place in scripture that spells out the message Paul was supposed to have received – and it was provided to us by the writer of Acts, a friend and admirer of Paul.[54] Paul himself says very little about his heavenly visit. In his letter to the Galatians (1:12), he reports he "received a revelation" from Jesus, and in 1 Corinthians 15:8, he mentions Jesus "appeared to him." He offers no further description of the event.

I don't know about you, but if something so amazing happened to me, I'd want to share all the juicy details. I couldn't help but wonder why Paul didn't give the incident more attention.

A Question of Timing

Another interesting fact that revealed itself in my research is that Paul's mystic experience took place approximately *three years* after Jesus had died and made his heavenly ascent (some Bible historians place it as late as six years). The question that kept coming up for me was why did Jesus wait so long to pay Paul a visit? Surely if Paul was indeed, as Ananias had indicated, "chosen by God to know his will" (Acts 22:14), it would have been much more efficacious to put him to work right away instead of giving him time to create an uproar in the community. Of course, in my past life as a Christian, I would have been satisfied with the idea that God's timing is not the same as ours. But in my new role of "truth-seeker," this action left me perplexed.

Why the Gentiles?

I was also puzzled as to why Jesus would send Paul to the Gentiles. In the gospel accounts, Jesus told his disciples to "Go nowhere among the Gentiles, and enter no town of the Samaritans, but go rather to the lost sheep of the house of Israel" (Matthew 10:5-6). Jesus also said about himself that he was "sent only to the lost sheep of the house of Israel" (Matthew 15:24). Why did Jesus change his mind?

Who Was Paul?

In my attempts to learn more about Paul, I could find only minimal information. There is no mention of him in secular history, and even the scriptures offer very little about his background.

In his own writings, Paul describes himself as an Israelite, of the stock of Abraham, of the tribe of Benjamin and stresses that before his visitation by Jesus, he was a strict follower of the law. In fact, he makes the statement, "as to the law, a Pharisee" (Philippians 3:5). Note that he does not come right out and say he is a Pharisee; rather, he follows the law *like* a Pharisee. I had never noticed this distinction, but my research revealed some scholars harbor doubts about Paul's Pharisaic claim. Hyam Maccoby[55] believes Paul made this claim in an attempt to sway his Jewish audience to his way of thinking (more on this later).

Any other personal information we have about Paul comes from the Book of Acts where the writer tells us that Paul was a

Jew, born in Tarsus, brought up in Jerusalem, and educated in ancestral law by Gamaliel (a respected Pharisaic teacher of the time). Some first-century historians doubt this last bit of information and believe it was included by the writer of Acts primarily to enhance Paul's credentials to the emerging church.

Modern-day scholars have described Paul as an eloquent writer, a powerful and charismatic orator, and an effective evangelist. Spong writes that he was a man of passion, power, commitment, and energy.[56] These descriptions seem appropriate since he was able to spread his concept of Jesus to hundreds of people during his lifetime and millions more after his death.

I also read that his teachings were a "mosaic of Jewish and heathen beliefs, doctrines, practices, traditions."[57] This last bit of information intrigued me. What did this mean? As I began to dig deeper, I soon discovered there was much more to this person named Paul than I ever learned in Sunday School.

Beyond The Biographical

Tarsus, the reported birthplace of Paul (and where he was most likely brought up), was located in the Diaspora.[58] Being Jews, his parents would have made sure he had an orthodox upbringing, including circumcision and regular study of the law and the prophets. He must have been an avid student because in his letters he brags that he has an above-average understanding of the Torah and the traditions of his faith (Galatians 1:14).

Paul would also have been exposed to Persian and Greek thinking and philosophies since Tarsus was one of the cities in the Mediterranean region that underwent the transition of rulers from Nebuchadnezzar, to Cyrus the Great, to Alexander the Great. Later, when he moved to Rome, he would also have been impacted by Roman ideologies. As we shall see, these influences played a major role in his later theology about Jesus.

God's People: The Jews

The Hebrew Bible (Old Testament) is a story about the Jews, God's Chosen People. It starts with God making a covenant with Abraham (Genesis 17:1-2) and continues with stories of their journey from the land of Egypt, the giving of the Ten Commandments, the many battles they had to fight to protect the land that God had given them, the various judges and kings that guided them, the loss of their land to the Babylonians and then the Persians, and finally the building of the second temple.

The Promise of a King

Probably one of the most far-reaching and debatable events in the history of the Jews is when God promises King David that one of his offspring would one day rule an everlasting kingdom. Over the years, this promised ruler came to be known to the Jewish people as the *mashiach*, a person (human being) specially appointed and empowered by God to usher in an era of peace and prosperity. The Jewish people often referred to this future time as the "End of Days" (*acharit ha-yamim*), or the Messianic Age.

The prophet Isaiah told the people that during this time there will be universal acceptance and worship of the one true God, hunger and illness will disappear, death will be "swallowed up forever," nations will recognize the wrongs they did to Israel, weapons of war will be destroyed, the earth will become abundant and fruitful, and sin and evil will be abolished.

It is important to note that in early Judaism, the End of Days did not involve cosmic events such as those predicted by the apocalyptic writers. It simply meant that God would send the *mashiach*, who would bring about the political and spiritual redemption of the Jewish people.

Could It Be ... ?

In the years immediately preceding the appearance of Jesus, the people had been living under Roman rule with its accompanying oppression and taxation. They felt hopeless and beaten down. There seemed to be no escape. The "arrogance of the privileged upper class and the rulers' contempt for Jewish piety and ancestral custom"[59] were almost more than they could bear.

Then Jesus arrives. In their desperate state, many see signs of the *mashiach* that God had told them about so long ago. Surely this was the one who would liberate Israel and restore the nation to its original greatness. Surely this was the one who would destroy the nations that had persecuted Israel for so long and set up the everlasting kingdom God had promised. The author of Luke's gospel clearly expresses the prevailing sentiment: "... we had hoped that he was the one to redeem Israel" (Luke 24:21).

Disappointment ... Then Hope

But something terrible happens. Jesus gets arrested ... and then he's crucified! How could this be? His followers, dejected and disappointed, scatter. The one they thought God had sent to deliver them was gone forever.

But wait!

Word spreads that Jesus has come back to life. Hope returns! It's even rumored that certain of his disciples saw him ascending to heaven to be with God, telling them he would one day return on "clouds of heaven" (Mark 14:62) to fulfill God's promise.

The followers are ecstatic! Their beliefs about him have been confirmed. They immediately get to work telling friends and relatives that the man known as *Yeshua* is the long-awaited *mashiach* and he's going to soon return to set up God's kingdom.

Before long, small groups of devoted believers form. They gather often in each other's homes to break bread and talk about Jesus, and they visit the Temple regularly to pray and await *apokatastasis pantōn,* the final establishment of all God has promised to Israel.

None of these people gave up their identity as Jews. They were still "God's People" as they continued to follow the Torah, perform circumcisions, keep the Sabbath, honor the Jewish festivals, and observe dietary laws and other Jewish customs. The only thing that differentiated them from other Jews is they now believed the establishment of God's kingdom was just around the corner and it would be ruled by Jesus. Others often referred to these groups as followers of "The Way," and considered James, the brother of Jesus, as the leader.

Not all first century Jews followed this pathway. Many did not accept Jesus as the messiah. For them, as well as for most present-day Jews, he did not fulfill the messianic prophecies for the *mashiach* as outlined in the Hebrew Scriptures.[60]

Paul's People: The Gentiles

Today, the primary meaning of the word *gentile* is "non-Jew" – people that are not part of the Jewish covenant with God. However, in the days of Paul, it also referred to *pagans*, those who worshipped Greek or Roman gods and goddesses.

The early pagan religions were many and varied and numerous shrines, temples, and statues were erected to honor the multitude of gods. Most of the religions were earth-based, which meant the followers had a high respect for nature. Worshippers regularly performed seasonal rituals and ceremonies to persuade the gods to ensure plentiful crops. They also sacrificed assorted domestic animals to appease their deities, and then shared a communal meal to enjoy the remains of the slain creature.

These were the Gentiles that Paul had been instructed to turn from "darkness to light." He faced a difficult task because none of these people had any use for the Jewish Torah or its purity and dietary restrictions. And even though they may have heard about Jesus, they certainly had no use for him or his teachings.

As a self-proclaimed strict follower of the law, I can imagine Paul feeling somewhat overwhelmed. How was he ever going to get these people to accept Jesus as the messiah? They had no stake in the future reestablishment of Israel as a nation. Not only that, they did not live by any moral codes, many believed in reincarnation, and they certainly did not believe in male circumcision!

How, in God's name, was he going to change their thinking? Yes indeed. Jesus had given Paul a very difficult assignment.

A Time for Contemplation

Paul writes in Galatians 1:17 that after his mystical experience, he left Damascus and headed for Arabia ("... I went away at once into Arabia ..."). He doesn't mention why he went there, but perhaps he needed time to sort things out and come up with a way to carry out his assigned task.

Something that Paul didn't immediately do, which I found puzzling, was to contact any of the members of the actual Jesus Movement. After becoming known for his actions against the early followers of Jesus, wouldn't he want to let them know he had changed? Apparently not, because approximately three years pass before Paul travels to Jerusalem. His visit is brief (15 days) and he doesn't meet with anyone but Cephas [Peter]. Rather offhandedly, he mentions he saw James, the brother of Jesus and the leader of the Jesus Movement (Galatians 1:18). I wondered why he didn't spend time with him as well.

Apparently, part of the reason Paul didn't feel it necessary to comingle with any members of the Jesus Movement is because he felt his "revelation" had placed him in a higher position than any of them (Galatians 1:11-12; 1 Corinthians 1:1). In fact, he went so far as to paint these original companions of Jesus as suspect ... even to the point that they should be "accursed" (Galatians 1:6-9) – condemned by God. Considering that these are the disciples who reportedly walked and talked with Jesus and heard his message firsthand, it seems incredulous that Paul would make such brash statements.

However, as we shall see, the theology about Jesus that Paul developed was decidedly different than what the early followers believed and taught. Could this be, as many of today's scholars believe, because Paul never met Jesus in person?

Paul's Solution

In his letters, Paul doesn't talk much about how he arrived at a solution for winning over the Gentiles. All we know is when he returned from his Arabian sojourn, he had devised a plan – one that differed radically from the teachings of Jesus. It was also a major departure from his Hebrew upbringing and the law that he so adamantly claimed to follow in his letter to the Philippians (3:4-6).

One of the first things Paul did was abolish the Torah as a requirement for salvation. This meant the Gentiles no longer had to worry about eating only certain types of food, following the Mosaic law, keeping the Sabbath, performing blood sacrifices, and observing Jewish festivals. Most importantly, they no longer had to abide by the most contentious part of Jewish law – male circumcision.

Then he took it a step further. He declared even the Jews did not need to abide by the Torah! (In fact, he even told them they were under a "curse" for following the law (Galatians 3:10), contradicting what God said in Deuteronomy 27:26: "Cursed be anyone who does not uphold the words of this law by observing them." I wondered where Paul got his authority to do this because throughout the Hebrew Bible, the people are admonished again and again by God's messengers to follow and live by the Torah. Not only that, Jesus himself never indicated the law was wrong and should be repealed. In fact, Matthew reports in 5:17 that Jesus said he came to *fulfill* the law and the teachings of the Prophets, not to abolish them. In verse 19, he adds that "whoever breaks one of the least of these commandments, and **teaches others to do the same**, will be called least in the kingdom of heaven" (emphasis added). Yet Paul ignored all this and confidently asserted that the time of the Torah is over.[61]

But Paul didn't stop there. Knowing that many of the Gentiles were members of the "Mystery Religions," he proceeded to formulate a religion that would appeal to them and ensure their acceptance of Jesus.

The Mystery Religions

In the centuries leading up to the birth of Christianity, various "Mystery Religions" spread and flourished throughout the ancient Mediterranean world.[62] There were "Outer Mysteries" (open to anyone) and "Inner Mysteries." To be admitted into the latter, individuals had to undergo a type of baptism (purification by water, fire, or air)[63] and perform certain rituals and ceremonies (e.g., fasting, confession of sins), all of which were held in secret.[64] Once accepted, the initiates believed they had exclusive access to divine revelations and truths. They also considered themselves to be set apart from the rest of the world. (Could this be why the author of John (15:19) told the Christians they *do not belong to the world*?)

At the core of these mystery religions was the belief in a dying-rising savior who sacrificed himself in order to give his followers eternal life. He was usually the offspring of a divine-human union and nearly always possessed special powers, including the ability to work miracles. After death, he either returned to life or triumphed over his enemies. (Remember, these religions were in place *before* Christianity.)

These "god-men" had many different names: in Egypt, he was Osiris; in Greece, Dionysus; in Asia Minor, Attis; in Syria, Adonis; and in Italy, Bacchus.[65] In the Greco-Roman communities where Paul preached, Mithras was the most popular god-man.

As I dug deeper, I was astonished – and a little unsettled – to discover how many similarities there were between these deities and Jesus. For example, mystery followers often called their god-man by such familiar titles as *light-bringer, healer, mediator, redeemer, savior, god's son, and deliverer.* They also used terms such as *sacrifice, salvation, resurrection,* and *immortality.*

But the most disconcerting information I uncovered was about the cult of Mithras, which, by the way, is said to have originated in Tarsus, Paul's reported birthplace. Following are several characteristics[66] of this god-man as listed by researchers who study ancient myths:[67, 68, 69]

> He was born on December 25th in a cave.
> His father was a god and his mother was a mortal virgin.
> He was considered a great traveling teacher and master.
> He had twelve companions or disciples.
> He performed miracles.
> His followers were baptized for their sins.
> He shared a last sacramental meal.
> He sacrificed himself to redeem humankind.
> He was buried in a tomb and rose after three days.

He was resurrected and ascended into heaven (his resurrection was celebrated every year).
His followers were promised immortality.
His holy day was Sun-Day (he was considered a sun god)

I couldn't believe I wasn't reading about Jesus! Yet these characteristics belonged to a figure that predated *Yeshua* by fourteen hundred years.

Probing further, I discovered that one of the primary goals of the mystery followers was to achieve union with their god-man through mystical experiences, which nearly always included a vision of a bright light. (Paul's visit from Jesus on the road to Damascus immediately came to mind.) Once they achieved this union, they believed the deity lived in them and they lived in the deity (Paul wrote to the Galatians that Christ lived in him, Galatians 2:20), and that they had been granted eternal life.

After reading this, I suddenly noticed how frequently Paul used the word *mystery* in his writings. He talked about the mystery of the gospel (Ephesians 6:19), the mystery that was hidden (Colossians 1:26), the mystery that was revealed to him (Ephesians 3:3), the mystery of Christ (Ephesians 3:4), and he describes the end-time resurrection as a mystery (1 Corinthians 15:51).

Each new bit of information further convinced me that Paul's exposure to (and possible membership in) the mystery religions helped him mold Jesus into an acceptable figure to the Gentiles. Even so, he still faced a major obstacle. He had to show them that *Yeshua* was somehow different from the other pagan gods. Otherwise, there would be no reason for them to switch camps.

Jesus' Makeover

To the followers of "the Way," Jesus was the human messiah God had promised. Although they were devastated after his untimely death, the reported after-death sightings revived their hopes and convinced them he would soon return to set up God's Kingdom.

To the mystery followers, Jesus was nothing more than a Jewish spiritual leader. His death was a mere blip on their radar. Their spiritual hopes for salvation and immortality rested in the mystical connections they formed with their various god-men. Knowing this, Paul began his crusade to reinvent Jesus and convince the Gentiles they could find what they were seeking in the resurrected man from Galilee.

What's in a Name?

Drawing from his Greek leanings, Paul began referring to Jesus as the *christos* (Christ), thereby removing the Hebrew title of *mashiach* (messiah). Although both words mean "anointed one," the use of the Greek title was more familiar to his intended converts and removed any reference to Jesus' "Jewishness." Some sources say *christos* also held the meaning of "one who is crowned with divinity."

Paul also knew the mystery religion followers referred to their deities as *kurios* ("lord" in Greek), so he further assisted his cause by frequently using this title when he talked about Jesus (*Lord Jesus Christ, Christ Jesus our Lord*).

The Resurrected Jesus

One of the many obstacles Paul faced in his efforts to win over the Gentiles is Jesus' resurrection. His Greco-Roman audience believed the soul/spirit was separate and distinct from the body. At death, the spirit lived on but the body ceased to exist; it did not return to any kind of physical life. Since Jesus was reportedly seen in actual bodily form after his death, Paul realized he must choose his words carefully.

He seemed to do this in his first letter to the Corinthians (the home of numerous mystery cults) where he went into great detail to convince his readers that after death the body is raised as a *spiritual* body. He compared the resurrected body to a seed of wheat or other grain that dies and then rises because this idea was familiar to these earth-based religions. He got even more explicit when he wrote that *flesh and blood cannot inherit the kingdom of God* (1 Corinthians 15:50).

He also used his visitation by Jesus (1 Corinthians 9:1) as an example and stressed that everyone will be *changed* (1 Corinthians 15:51). It is clear he wanted to convince the Gentiles that his resurrected Christ possessed not only an immortal spirit, but also a *transfigured* body.

Eventually, he was able to establish the doctrine that exists today: a combination of the Greek belief in an eternal soul and the Jewish belief in a bodily resurrection.[70]

Jesus Saves

At the heart of Christianity is the belief that salvation comes through believing in Jesus and his atoning death on the cross. **Few are aware this doctrine was never mentioned, promoted, or taught by Jesus himself**. Nor is it addressed anywhere in the Hebrew Bible. (Old Testament scriptures used by church leaders today to corroborate Paul's teachings are "after the fact" and did not hold the same meaning to the ancient Jews.)

In today's churches, the accepted method for redemption is based entirely on the theology that Paul developed so the Gentiles "may receive forgiveness of sin."

In the Matter of Sin

When Paul abolished the Torah to satisfy the Gentiles, he essentially took away the Jewish guidelines for life (Leviticus 18:5). How would they now be able to please God? For centuries they had been taught that salvation came through following the Mosaic law. Paul knew this since, by birth, he was a Jew. But his mystic revelation had changed his outlook, in more ways than one.

He now believed, and taught, that the law was not the answer. In his view, the law did not have the power to save; this could only be accomplished by believing in his Christ's death and resurrection. This was an easy pill to follow for Paul's Gentile followers. All they had to do was symbolically die and rise with Jesus to achieve salvation – no different than what they did with their other gods.

Convincing the Jews the Mosaic law was now defunct was a much more difficult task, so he developed the "original sin" doctrine (that exists today and can *only* be traced to Paul). He told them sin was in the world *before* the law was given (Romans 5:13) – and it was all because of Adam's wrongdoing in the Garden of Eden (Romans 5:12). He further asserted that with sin came death, and since *all have sinned and fall short of the glory of God* (Romans 3:23), the only way to life and salvation was by acknowledging that Jesus was the Messiah/Savior. (The first theologian to further this teaching was St. Augustine.[71])

For most first-century Jews, Paul's position was totally antithetical. According to early Judaic teachings (*and* maintained in modern-day Judaism), everyone is born innocent; that is, they enter the world free of sin.[72] Throughout life, people may make choices that lead to sin, but it is not part of their inherent nature. To the Jews, sin is a violation of the divine commandments and is seen as an *act* (thought, word, or deed), not a "state of being"[73] or part of the human condition. Further, God explained in

Ezekiel (18:20) that sinners will be punished for their own sins, not for the sins of others.

All this made me wonder where Paul, born a Jew and trained in ancestral law, got the idea that sin was genetically inherited.

The Dream of Immortality

Since Paul was fully aware the mystery followers believed they must join with and become one with their gods in order to find salvation and gain immortality, he frequently reinforced the deity of his Christ. He wanted to make sure they viewed him in the same light as Mithras and other familiar god-men.

To the Philippians (2:6), he wrote that Jesus came "in the form of God," he told the Colossians (2:9) that the "whole fullness of deity dwells bodily" in him (Christ), he shared with the Corinthians (2 Corinthians 4:4) that Christ is the "image of God," and in Titus (2:13), he explicitly pointed out that Jesus is "our great God and Savior."

In his letter to the Romans, he emphasized that eternal life would be theirs when they believed in and joined with his Christ (Romans 6:23). He even used himself as an example (1 Timothy 1:16). He further expanded on this thought when he wrote to the Philippians (1:21) that for him, "living is Christ and dying is gain."

Paul further advanced his cause by telling the Gentiles that Christ is "within" (2 Corinthians 13:5; Colossians 1:27). He knew they would interpret this as the mystical union that takes their spirit into the afterlife.

Full Acceptance

The Gentiles originally were "strangers to the covenants of promise" (Ephesians 2:12), but Paul, on the authority of a light from heaven, gave them full standing by proclaiming: "There is no longer Jew or Greek, there is no longer slave or free, there is no longer male or female; for all of you are one in Christ Jesus" (Galatians 3:28).

And The Winner Is ...

History has proven that Paul's persuasions were enormously compelling. By effectively divorcing his newly formed religion from its Jewish roots, he swayed thousands of Gentiles to his Christ. The church that evolved is entirely Gentile and any Jew who becomes Christian loses his Jewish identity and becomes a Gentile himself.[74]

Why did Paul's form of Christianity flourish and the Jesus Movement disappear? Primarily due to Paul's relentless zeal to accomplish the mission that he believed a spiritualized Jesus had given to him. Paul's religion was simple to join, had a central figure that bore a strong resemblance to the mystery religion saviors, offered the reward of immortality simply through believing in Christ, removed dietary and circumcision restrictions, and made few demands on its followers. It appealed to the Hellenized Jews as well as the pagans. No wonder it succeeded. As Barrie Wilson wrote, Paul had a "winning marketing formula."[75]

Final Thoughts

Many Christians feel a special connection with Paul. They tend to see him as the shining example of a model Christian. Indeed, his teachings ... his writings ... his doctrines make up the mainstay of the Christian church. In fact, it could be said that if it hadn't been for Paul, there would be no Christianity.

Unfortunately, because so few take the time and energy to look beyond what they have been told, they fail to see the true results of Paul's actions. In his fervor to fulfill the mission he believed came from a disembodied Jesus, he transformed *Yeshua*, God's messenger to the Jews, into a deity figure recognizable only to the Gentiles. He taught doctrines and concepts that Jesus never mentioned and created a religion that Jesus would not have recognized.

I cannot help but feel regret that the teachings of Jesus were smothered by the teachings of Paul. If people had only followed the simple message of love that Jesus shared, there might not be the divisions, disagreements – even wars – that have existed throughout history for the past two thousand plus years.

We would do well to put aside the teachings of Paul and instead imitate the wisdom, kindness, and forgiving spirit imparted by *Yeshua* during his time on this earth.

5. THE BIG BAD GUY: Is He For Real?

"Somehow our devils are never quite what we expect when we meet them face to face."
  – Nelson DeMille

"The invisible and the non-existent look very much alike."
  – Huang Po

You have probably heard the phrase, "The devil made me do it!" Often used by someone who has been caught in an awkward situation, it helps to relieve the tension of the moment, nearly always brings a laugh, and is a great way to redirect blame.

However, not everyone takes the concept of the devil so lightheartedly. Many followers of the Bible believe he is the Big Bad Guy, i.e., *Satan* – a very real entity whose primary goal is to disrupt people's lives and cause them to sin against God. They are convinced he is the leader of a group of demons (angels that rebelled against God), and will one day face God in a horrific end time battle referred to as Armageddon.

I was once one of those people. During my Christian years, the image of a malevolent, wicked, unholy creature was always with me. I may not have lived in daily fear, but the underlying dread was there. Even though church leaders told me I was "safe" in Christ, I couldn't shake the frightening thoughts of what might happen if I didn't keep this evil beast at bay.

Even after I left Christianity, I was unable to disengage myself from the grasp of the Big Bad Guy. Although less of a threat, he refused to go away. It wasn't until I began writing this book and learning about the history of "Satan" that I was finally able to free my mind and spirit from his fearsome power.

If you live with this same foreboding, hopefully what I uncovered about the so-called "prince of darkness" will help to allay your fears and bring you a sense of peace.

Wherefore Art Thou, Satan?

Many, if not most, Christians are unaware that "Satan," the embodiment of evil, **does not exist**. Now before you think I'm coming from somewhere out in left field, let me assure you this conclusion came only after many hours of extensive research. It required examining what I had always been told with a critical eye and applying what some might call "common sense." It was a *very* difficult task. Probably the hardest part was overcoming the idea that it was actually "Satan" manipulating my mind and making me *believe* he wasn't real. Nonetheless, I kept moving forward until I was able to rip out the deeply-rooted beliefs and see the truth.

The Game of the Name

Among today's Christians, the Big Bad Guy is known by many names. Besides Satan or Devil, he is also known as the Evil One, Prince of Darkness, Lucifer, Father of Lies, Destroyer, God of this World, Great Deceiver, Prince of Demons, Man of Sin, the Enemy, Liar, Tempter, Master of Deceit, Lord of Death, just to name a few. Less familiar names are Azazel, Semihazah, Mastema, Beliar, Sammael, and Beelzebub.

Some believe he is the *Serpent* in the Garden of Eden, the *Fallen Angel* mentioned in Isaiah, and the *Beast/Dragon* talked about in the Book of Revelation. Others believe certain kings mentioned in the Old Testament are representations of the Big Bad Guy; e.g., King of Tyre and King of Babylon.

With such an array of impressive titles, it is apparent that "Satan" holds an important place in Christianity. But does he deserve it? Let's look closer.

The Hebrew Satan

In the ancient Hebrew language, there is no "Satan" (proper name). There is, however, "the satan," which is a literal translation of the Hebrew word, *ha-satan*. When Jewish scholars produced the Septuagint, the Greek translation of the Torah, they translated *ha-satan* to *diabolos* (which is where we get the English title of "devil").

Throughout the Hebrew Scriptures, the term *ha-satan* was generally used to describe an adversary (as in war). Some examples: In 1 Samuel 29:4, the Philistines fear King David may become *ha-satan* (an adversary); in 2 Samuel 19:22, David tells the sons of Zeruiah they have become *ha-satans* (adversaries); and in 1 Kings 5:4, Solomon comments that there are no longer any *ha-satans* (adversaries) standing in the way so he can move forward with building the temple. Occasionally, the word was used to depict an opponent (one who puts obstacles in the way) or an accuser (one who points out misbehavior).

In each of the above examples, *ha-satan* is referring to a human being; however, there are a few instances when an angel has served as "the satan." One such occurrence is recorded in Numbers 22:22 where God put an obstacle (*the angel of the Lord*) in Balaam's way to block his travels. Another is in the story of Job (see below).

Things Are Not Always As They Seem

In 1 Chronicles 21:1, there is a passage where *ha-satan* is used but most Bibles show it as "Satan" (personal pronoun). This has caused considerable confusion among some believers because they think it is referring to the Big Bad Guy. Few are aware there is a parallel passage in 2 Samuel 24:1 that indicates "the Lord" is the one who incites David to count the people of Israel and Judah. Are we to say that the Lord is the Evil One? God forbid!

In order to clear up this disparity, we need to know when each of these books was written. The second book of Samuel is believed to have been written sometime in the ninth century BCE; whereas 1 Chronicles was produced sometime after 450 BCE. Why does this make a difference? Because the latter was written during the Persian Period, that two hundred year span when the Israelites came under Zoroastrian influence (532-330 BCE) and the personification of "the adversary" had begun.

The fact of the matter is that scholars who study ancient languages have found **zero** verses in the Old Testament where *ha-satan* is referring to the familiar fellow so many know today as the ruler of a fiery hell.

Is That You, Satan?

OK, this all seemed to make sense, but I was still faced with a big stumbling block. What about the Book of Job? My bible clearly states that "Satan" was the guy behind Job's problems. And what about Lucifer, the fallen angel that Isaiah writes about? Or the serpent in the Garden of Eden? And isn't Ezekiel describing a renegade angel? According to what I had been taught, all these were examples of the Big Bad Guy. I needed to dig a little deeper.

Job and His Heavenly Accuser

In the prologue of Job's book, we are told that "Satan" joined some angels (heavenly beings) for a meeting with God (Job 1:6). Surprisingly, it seemed to be a fairly friendly encounter – certainly not what you would expect if this was the Big Bad Guy! It took only a little investigation to discover why. The word used here is exactly the same as the examples cited previously; that is, *ha-satan*. In fact, there is a footnote in nearly every English Bible that indicates the more literal translation is "accuser."[76]

CHAPTER 5. THE BIG BAD GUY: IS HE FOR REAL?

So why was the title of "Satan" used in this book instead of accuser or adversary as in other Bible passages? As with the example in 1 Chronicles, it probably has to do with when the book was written. There is considerable variance between Old Testament scholars, but many believe the Book of Job was authored during the post-exilic period when *ha-satan* was slowly transforming into a distinct personality, primarily due to Zoroastrian influence.

However, this still didn't explain why God allowed *ha-satan* to wreak havoc on Job's life. With a little more delving, I learned that this particular "accuser" had a special function in God's divine court. It was his job to "go to and fro on the earth" and look for any signs of disloyalty among humans and then report on them to his Supervisor. Elaine Pagels describes him as a "roving intelligence agent."[77] Several other sources call him "God's prosecuting attorney." The important thing to note is that it was *not* his job to stir up trouble, just to report on it. He worked *for* God, not *against* God.

During this particular heavenly meeting, the adversary speculates about Job's dedication and commitment. He points out that it's easy to be faithful when someone lives such a charmed life. God disagrees, but decides to *allow* the accuser to test Job. Important note: the "Satan" in this story is not an independent agent. He is a member of God's heavenly court and *must have God's permission* before he can do anything.

Many in the scholarly field contend the Book of Job is nothing more than a type of "folk tale" (parable, fable, allegory) written to assure the Israelites living during the terrible times of the Exile that God remained faithful. Evangelical Christians, on the other hand, prefer to see the story as totally true with Job as a prototype of Jesus (the "Man of Sorrows") and *the satan* as the supernatural Big Bad Guy harassing a faithful man of God.

Lucifer, A Shining Star

After dispelling the idea that it wasn't actually the Big Bad Guy at work in the story of Job, I still had questions about "Lucifer." According to a long-held belief in Christian circles, "Satan" is actually an angel who exalted himself above God and was subsequently thrown out of heaven. This persuasion seems to come from a passage in Isaiah (14:12-20) where, in the very popular King James Version of the Bible, verse 12 reads, "How art thou fallen from heaven, O Lucifer, son of the morning!"

The belief is further enhanced by a scripture in the Gospel of Luke where Jesus purportedly said he saw Satan fall from heaven like a flash of lightning (Luke 10:17-18). Putting two and two together, many have concluded he must have been talking about the "Lucifer" in Isaiah.

In truth, the word used in the original text of Isaiah was *hilel*, a Hebrew word that means "morning star" or "the shining one." When Jerome prepared the Vulgate (Latin) edition of the Bible in the early fifth century (from which the King James Version originated), he translated *hilel* to *Lucifer*, which means "shining" or "light bringer." Even though most Bible translations have discontinued the use of Lucifer and instead use terms such as "star of the morning," "Day Star," "son of Dawn," or "shining one" in this portion of scripture, a large number of Christians cling to the King James translation, believing that Satan and Lucifer are one and the same.[78]

Beyond the translation difficulties, a careful read of verse 4 in Isaiah makes it abundantly clear he is not writing about a fallen angel at all. He is clearly referring to the King of Babylon (Isaiah 14:4), who not only persecuted the children of Israel, but had also come to think of himself as a God. Isaiah is writing that the king will violently be removed from his throne and sent to *sheol* (the place of the dead, not "hell" as some Bible readers assume) where he will be covered with worms and mocked by people because he has no more power.

Some readers might be surprised to learn that in the Book of Revelation there is a scripture where Jesus refers to *himself* as the "bright morning star" (Revelation 22:16). Does this mean he is the Big Bad Guy? I would venture to say the faithful would reply with a resounding "No!"

So where did the tradition originate that Isaiah was writing about God's antagonist? It seems to have come from the teachings of two early theologians, i.e., Origen of Alexandria[79] (c. 185-254 CE) and Tertullian (c. 155-225 CE). Origen was the first to declare "Satan" was a renegade angel,[80] and Tertullian amplified this idea. Their exegeses seem to have been derived from books written during the Intertestamental Period, such as First Enoch and Jubilees (discussed later).

The Egotistical Angel

Yet another instance in which I was told the Bible was talking about the Big Bad Guy is in Ezekiel (28:1-19). Even though the words "devil", "satan", or "fallen angel" are nowhere to be found in this section of scripture, numerous Christians are certain Ezekiel is writing about "someone" other than the person named in verse 12 (the king of Tyre). In fact, many point to this story and state with complete certainty that it is all about how "Satan" got his start and how his pride and sinful nature will eventually bring about his demise.

But is this section of scripture *really* about the Big Bad Guy? Or is it an inference prompted by the teachings of church leaders? And if the latter, where did the whole idea originate?

First, it's important to note this section of scripture was written during the Babylonian captivity (593-565 BCE). As previously discussed, the Israelites had lost their temple and began to question *Yahweh's* role in what was happening. Ezekiel, who is considered one of the Major Prophets (messengers from God), felt the burden to ensure his people that even in defeat and despair, God was still in control. He also reprimanded them for being rebellious and stubborn, but the most significant part of the book is when he passes judgment not only on the king of Tyre, but also on the kings/nations of Ammon, Moab, Edom, Philistia, Sidon, and Egypt.

Since Ezekiel was speaking to *several* foreign rulers, I wondered why Christians isolate the message to the leader of Tyre and assign it a hidden/second meaning. It clearly states in verse 2 (and again in verse 9) that Ezekiel is speaking to a *mortal*, yet for some mysterious reason, believers are certain everything changes in verse 12 and the scriptures are now directed to an egotistical angel.

I spent considerable time looking for an answer. In the process, I came across a translation of the original Hebrew text and discovered something interesting. In verse 13, many Bibles state that king Tyre was "in Eden, the garden of God" (inferring to some that he was the serpent/Satan in Genesis 3). However, the original Hebrew word that has been translated as "Eden" actually means "luxury." So the correct wording is: "In the luxury of the garden of God."[81] Or according to another source: "You come into luxury, a paradise from Elohim."[82] Ezekiel is accusing the king of living in luxury; he is not stating the king was in the Edenic garden of Genesis.

I now felt confident that Ezekiel was not writing about the Big Bad Guy, but there was still one big question swirling around in my head. Where did this belief originate in the first place? And how did it gain such a firm foothold in Christian circles?

After intense research, I came to the conclusion it was based on the writings of Origen of Alexandria (mentioned earlier). It was his belief that Ezekiel could not possibly be talking about a human being and therefore must be referring to "some superior power which had fallen away from a higher position,"[83] and who was then converted into a "wicked being."

It is important to recognize this interpretation came from a man who was highly educated in Platonic philosophy and studied pagan Greek wisdom. Even so, Origen played a major role in the formation of Christian doctrine. His viewpoint on this matter set a precedent in early Christianity and remains the accepted teaching in a number of evangelical churches. A good illustration of this is in Moody's Handbook of Theology,[84] a "textbook" used by many Christian leaders, where it is written:

> *Satan's original state. Ezekiel 28:12-15 describes Satan prior to his fall. He enjoyed an exalted position in the presence of God; the brilliance of heaven was his surrounding (28:13). He was called the "anointed…covering cherub" who enjoyed the position of highest honor before God (28:14,16).*
>
> *Satan's fall. Satan's fall is described in both Ezekiel 28 and Isaiah 14. Because of his sin Satan was cast down from the presence of God (Ezek. 28:16). The reason for Satan's downfall was his pride; his heart was lifted up because of his beauty, and his wisdom became corrupt (28:17). The statement indicates Satan must have had extraordinarily high rank that led to his pride.*

I must admit I struggled with accepting that Ezekiel's message was meant for the ruler of Tyre. The Christian perspective of these verses was firmly embedded within my belief system. However, after a thorough investigation, I could no longer see anything sinister in Ezekiel's writings. Scripture states he was speaking to a human being (mortal) and I found no evidence to believe otherwise.

The Crafty Serpent

Of all the stories in the Bible that relate to "Satan," I find the one about the serpent in the Garden of Eden the most creative. Throughout my research, I came across numerous dissertations by the faithful about what "really" happened during the meeting between the serpent and Eve ... and why. Again and again I read, practically word-for-word, what I had been taught during my Christian experience. The fact that there is little to no basis for this oft-repeated tale seems to matter little to the various expositors.

According to tradition, the downfall of humankind started because Eve, after a *talking serpent* told her that God was lying about eating a certain fruit in the Garden, went ahead and ate it and also gave some to Adam, her husband (Genesis 3:1-6). (On the surface, can anyone deny there isn't at least a minimal amount of incredulity in this story?) After the first couple confessed they had shared the fruit, the Bible tells us God cursed the serpent and proclaimed it must forever crawl on its belly and eat dust. Nowhere does it say that God turned the serpent into an evil spirit.

In the original Hebrew language, the word for serpent is *nahash* and this is the word used in Genesis, not *ha-satan*. So where did the belief that the serpent was a representation of "Satan" get started?

During the period between 200 BCE and 200 CE, there were numerous "books" circulating among the early Jewish communities that were (falsely) attributed to biblical figures and times of the past. Modern scholars consider most of these works spurious and refer to them as *pseudepigrapha* (a Greek term meaning "falsely inscribed"). Most believe it is in this late Jewish literature that the serpent became identified with the devil.

A good example is in the book called "Life of Adam and Eve,"[85] which is seen as an ancient biographical sketch of the first couple. In it, the (anonymous) author reports that "Satan" has a conversation with the serpent: "Then he [Satan] went and summoned the serpent and said to him, 'Arise, come to me so that I may enter into you and speak through your mouth as much as I will need to say.' At that time the serpent became a lyre for him ..."[86]

The story continues with the serpent "talking" to Eve. He asks her what they are doing in the garden and she replies that God had told them to guard the garden. "Satan" then asks Eve, through the mouth of the serpent, if they eat from all the trees in the garden. Eve answers by explaining that God told them they could not eat from the tree in the middle of the garden or they would die. The serpent/Satan assures her she will not die. As the story goes, Eve "listens" to the serpent and goes ahead and eats the fruit of the forbidden tree and then shares a bite with Adam. (Remember, this conversation is not from the Bible.)

It is apparent this identification of "Satan" and the serpent became part of the early Christians' belief system when we consider the words of two New Testament writers. In 2 Corinthians 11:3, Paul writes that the *serpent* deceived Eve. (Since he provides no further comments or explanation, he must have known his readers would be familiar with the earlier stories.) And the author of Revelation leaves little doubt that he believes the serpent and "Satan" are one and the same (Revelation 12:9, 20:2).

What really cinched "Satan's" role in the Garden of Eden seems to have come from Justin Martyr (c. 100-165 CE), an early Christian apologist.[87] According to Henry Ansgar Kelly,[88] Justin was the "first person to postulate Satan's responsibility for inducing the fall of Adam and Eve." Kelly remarks that Justin didn't provide any reasons for this claim; he simply identified

"Satan" with the serpent. Irenaeus (second century bishop of Lyons) also claims in his writings (*Against Heresies*) that Eve was deceived by the "Satan" hidden in the serpent.

Augustine of Hippo, a more contemporary church father (354-430 CE) and another one of mainstream Christianity's greatest influencers,[89] wrote in *The Literal Meaning of Genesis*: "This serpent, however, could be called the wisest of the beasts not by reason of its irrational soul but rather because of another spirit – that of the Devil – dwelling in it."[90] (Provocative side note: Augustine was greatly influenced by Neo-Platonism, a pagan philosophy that includes elements of metaphysical thought, mysticism, theosophy, and theurgy, i.e., "white magic".)

A point of interest is that the serpent is one of the oldest and most widespread mythological symbols.[91] In some cultures, serpents are positive (e.g., Buddhism[92]); in others (e.g., Christianity), they are negative. Based on how viewed, various characteristics are assigned to them. Some are considered deceitful and vindictive, while others are seen as symbols of knowledge. Some are utilized as guardians of temples and other sacred places. They are depicted as dragons (Revelations), sea serpents (Leviathan, a demon described in Job), and are connected in more than one culture to a tree; e.g., Tree of Life, Tree of Knowledge, Tree of Immortality, Tree of Enlightenment, etc. In the Zoroastrian religion, the principle of evil (*Ahriman*) was symbolized by a serpent.

For me, the well-established belief that "Satan" was play-acting as a snake in the Garden of Eden is simply not credible. Besides, there is nothing in the Genesis scripture that indicates *ha-satan* was anywhere in or around the Garden.

CHAPTER 5. THE BIG BAD GUY: IS HE FOR REAL?

Mistaken Identity

It seems clear, at least to me, that it was not "Satan" lurking in the shadows of the Old Testament. In fact, his supposed presence reminds me of the familiar boogeyman that lives under the bed or in the closet. Once you shine a light into his hiding spot, you discover nothing is there.

The premise changes, however, when we move into the New Testament. Here, the Big Bad Guy stands squarely at center stage. What happened? How did *ha-satan*, the adversary, gain such a starring role? As we shall see, his entourage included some very persuasive agents.

Satan Moves into the Spotlight

The transformation of "Satan" from bit player to superstar came about during the so-called "silent years" – the approximate three to four hundred year gap between the end of the Hebrew sacred writings and the appearance of Jesus (often called the "Second Temple" period). This is when the Jewish people went through the tumultuous times of the Babylonian captivity, the Persian and Greek takeovers, the unholy desecration of the Jewish temple by the Greek ruler Antiochus Epiphanes, and the oppression of Roman rule.

The people struggled with their faith through these years. They tried to hang on to the promises God had made to them, but it was becoming more and more difficult as foreign nations deprived them of their heritage and independence. The teachings of the Persian Zoroastrians – that an evil spirit was behind their troubles – became more and more attractive. An awareness and sensitivity to the supernatural began to develop and grow. Add to that the Greek philosophy that a group of divine beings (*daemons*) were the cause of evil in the world and we begin to get a few glimpses on how "Satan" began his ascent to stardom.

However, it was the apocalyptic (revelatory, prophetic) authors mentioned in Chapter Two that had the greatest influence on the changing status of "Satan." As you may recall, these individuals reportedly received visions and messages from angelic sources about the ultimate destiny of humankind.

The writings were a blend of reality and fantasy. Nearly all of them contained predictions of end-time events, including cosmic battles between good and evil, a resurrection of the dead, a day of judgment, the meting out of rewards and punishment, the creation of a new world, and of course, the arrival of a messianic hero who would defeat the enemies of Israel. Many of the tales included cryptic descriptions of monstrous, bizarre beasts (the familiar book of Daniel, said to have been written during this period, is an excellent example) and transcendental visits to heaven and the underworld.[93]

What was most significant about these works is the way the authors began to develop a cosmic entity (based on myths from surrounding cultures as well as their own creativity) that could be blamed for all the bad things that were happening. Or as Wray and Mobley put it, they began revealing a "cosmic conspiracy" led by a "supernatural criminal mastermind" who controlled a vast network of demonic forces.[94]

We can be reasonably certain these "books" were quite popular among the Jewish people during this period, not only because they provided hope in a time of political unrest, but the shadowy concept of a dark antithetical force allowed them to preserve their belief in God's goodness. (By the time of the New Testament writers, this "shadowy concept" had become a full-fledged belief.)

Best Sellers

Two widely circulated books that seem to have helped "Satan" rise to stardom were the Book of Enoch[95] (also called

First Enoch) and the Book of Jubilees.[96] Although neither book was included in the canonized New Testament, both were instrumental in the development of the idea of "Satan" as the Principle Power of Evil. In fact, one New Testament scholar commented the Book of Enoch contributed significantly to "intertestamental views of angels, heaven, judgment, resurrection, and the Messiah." He added that it had "left its stamp upon many of the NT writers, especially the author of Revelation."[97]

One story in Enoch's book that I found particularly significant was about some "bad" (i.e., fallen) angels (called "Watchers"[98]) who were led by *Azazel* (as previously noted, this is one of "Satan's" many aliases). According to the author, these "Watchers" leave heaven to mate with the "daughters of men" and end up producing the *Nephilim*, a hybrid race of giants. These offspring eventually turn on humankind and create violence, corruption, and death. Fortunately, God sends "good" angels to put a stop to the troublemakers. Azazel is then bound hand and foot and thrown into darkness until the "day of great judgment" when he will be "cast into the fire." (Could this be where the author of Revelation got his inspiration in 20:10?) The author of Enoch then writes: "Because the whole earth has been corrupted through the works that were taught by Azazel: to him **ascribe all sin** (emphasis added).[99] (Christian tradition teaches that "Satan" is the author and instigator of sin.) God then directs "Michael"[100] to bind Azazel's "associates" for seventy generations in the valleys of the earth, until the day of their judgment when they will be led off to the "abyss of fire."[101]

The Book of Jubilees includes a similar story, except the angels who leave heaven do so for benevolent reasons. Their task is to teach humans justice and righteousness; however, this soon changes as the angels begin to lust after the daughters of men. Another difference is the leader is known as *Mastema* (another of

"Satan's" aliases) and his outcome varies slightly from the account in First Enoch. Rather than being cast into a pit to await final judgment, Mastema implores God to allow him to keep one-tenth of his cohorts so he can "execute the power of [his] will upon the sons of men."[102] God grants his request and sends the rest of the evil spirits to a place of darkness and condemnation. Mastema then takes over the role of inducing humans to sin.

Both of these stories seem to be a reworking of a passage in Genesis (6:1-2, 4). In the Bible account, the "sons of God" (*bene elohim*) join with the "daughters of man" (*benot ha-adam*) and produce children. The scriptures offer no direct evidence that the Nephilim were the offspring of this union, nor is there any mention of them creating havoc. In fact, they are referred to in the last part of verse four as "heroes that were of old, warriors of renown."

Nonetheless, it seems both of these writers saw things differently. To them, the "sons of God" were fallen angels and "Satan" was the malefic instigator behind the event. Based on my Christian teachings, this is the interpretation that dominates today, most likely bolstered by two New Testament epistles (2 Peter 2:4 and Jude 6) that include references to "sinning angels" being cast into hell and committed to chains.

A couple of things perplexed me about these accounts – where did the writers get the idea it was angels who mated with the humans? Angels are generally considered to be spiritual beings, and therefore not reproductively compatible with human women. Also, nowhere in Genesis (or anywhere else in the Hebrew Scriptures) are angels called the "sons of God." Many Christian theologians attempt to correlate the two, but I could find no valid evidence that states they are one and the same.

Also Widely Read

Another very popular book during this period was the *Life of Adam and Eve* (previously referenced). In my research, I came across the following translation that seems to contribute to the idea common in Christian circles that "Satan" was cast out of heaven because of his pride. This writer seems to feel it had something to do with the Big Bad Guy's refusal to be subservient to Adam:

And I [Satan] answered [Michael], "I do not worship Adam....I will not worship one inferior and subsequent to me. I am prior to him in creation; before he was made, I was already made. He ought to worship me." When they heard this, other angels who were under me refused to worship him. And Michael asserted, "Worship the image of God. But if now you will not worship, the Lord God will be wrathful with you." And I said, "If he be wrathful with me, I will set my throne above the stars of heaven and will be like the Most High." And the Lord was angry with me and sent me with my angels out from our glory; and because of you, we were expelled into this world from our dwellings and have been cast onto the earth. (Life of Adam and Eve 14-16)

These accounts are excellent examples of how the "story behind the story" developed. Imaginative writers selected familiar tales, added their own spin, and passed them around the neighborhood. What I find amazing is that Christian leaders who assert the Bible is the inspired word of God use these (and other) *extra-biblical* texts as source material to justify the Big Bad Guy's existence.

From Abstract to Avatar

Probably the most significant indication that the Big Bad Guy was becoming more than an idea was found in the *War Scrolls*, discovered among the Dead Sea Scrolls. Most scholars believe these documents were created by the Essenes, a first-century, ultra-orthodox, secretive Jewish group. From all indications, it appears the Essenes saw "Satan" as a very real personality who commanded a legion of followers in heaven and on earth, and who was engaged in a cosmic battle with God. (Sound familiar?) They were certain he had "taken over" many of God's people and turned them into allies. They called themselves the "sons of light" and felt it was their responsibility to wage war against this evil despot of darkness.

And the Oscar Goes To ...

With help from his enthusiastic promoters, "Satan" had now moved from bit player to full-fledged star. The entire community of New Testament writers couldn't stop talking about him (according to one source,[103] the "Devil" and/or demons are mentioned no less than 568 times). Interestingly, there is no discussion of his origin; he simply "appears." Of course, we now know there was no need because the people had become well acquainted with Mr. Bad Guy through the apocalyptic writers.

Even Jesus was acutely aware of "Satan" and his propensity for no good. According to the gospel writers, Jesus refers to him as the *evil one* in the parable of the weeds (Matthew 13:38-39), indicates he has a kingdom (Matthew 12:26), states that he kept a woman in bonds for eighteen years (Luke 13:16), describes him as the *ruler of this world* (John 14:30; John 12:31), and calls him a murderer and liar (John 8:44).

Paul also spoke often of "Satan" and cautioned his followers to constantly be on the lookout for this wily one (2 Corinthians 2:11, 4:4, 11:15; Ephesians 4:27, 6:11).

And of course we can't forget the book of Revelation where "Satan" takes on his grandest role as the Chief Antagonist who does battle with the rider of the white horse, (generally viewed by the faithful as being Jesus). Similar to the earlier stories, he eventually ends up in the lake of fire. This time, however, Christian tradition teaches this will be his "final hurrah."

The Beat Goes On

Over the years, the Big Bad Guy has continued to stay in the limelight. In the early fourteenth century, Dante wrote about him in the epic poem, *Inferno*. Later (1667), in *Paradise Lost and Regained*, John Milton solidified "Satan" as the leader of the fallen angels and turned him into a mighty warlord, hell bent on destroying man. Although both were works of fiction, they helped to expand and reinforce beliefs about the Big Bad Guy among the people of the time, as well as future generations.

Of course, we can't forget *The Exorcist*, a 1973 horror film about the demonic possession of a young girl. This movie, one of a cycle of "demonic child" films produced in the late 1960s and early 1970s, had a significant influence on popular culture. It was considered by many as one of the scariest movies of all time.

Even in today's world, "Satan" has "star" status. While some see him as nothing more than a symbol of evil, others view him as a very real (and very scary) living being. This is particularly true among conservative Christians. In fact, the following was published by a Baptist organization in a 1993 article: "Any system of religious belief that denies the **literal reality** and actual personality of Satan is radically unChristian and unBiblical in nature and clearly under the dominion of the very devil whom it denies"[104] (emphasis added).

Final Thoughts

After poring through scores of books, websites, and the Bible itself, I have concluded the "Devil" is nothing more than a figment of imagination. Early Jewish writers created him to help people understand the evil that was happening all around them during the post-exilic period. Since they could not, in good conscience, place the blame for their problems on *Yahweh*, these creative individuals devised a supernatural entity to be the fall guy. No longer was *ha-satan* simply God's prosecutor, intelligence agent, or helper. He had become "Satan," the Enemy of God's people.

While not everyone (e.g., the Pharisees) accepted the notion of a great supernatural power hostile to God,[105] the groups that did exerted strong influence over their fellow countrymen. This was particularly true among the early Christians who repeatedly invoked the imagery of "Satan" in order to disparage or demonize those who refused to believe in Jesus as the Christ. Unfortunately, the same holds true today.

Over time, the personhood and power of "Satan" has grown even more. Today, there are those who believe he actually has the ability to "possess" individuals and control their actions. And many look with fear and dread towards an unknown time in the future when "Satan" will take on human form as the "Antichrist."

Exit Stage Left

More than any other, the Christian concept of the "Devil" was one of the hardest for me to shake. I had been so indoctrinated with the idea of his power and influence, I actually faced this chapter with fear and dreading. However, I can no longer credit a supernatural entity with being the source of all evil. To do so is to accept a myth – a traditional story that explains the worldview of people who lived long ago in a world much different than ours.

There is only one Supreme Being of the universe. There is no dualism. There is no battle being waged between two powerful supernatural entities. To believe anything different is to cast doubt on what God declares in Isaiah 45:6: ... *there is no one besides me. I am the Lord, and there is no other.*

Chapter 5. The Big Bad Guy: Is He For Real?

"Satan" does not exist.

6. HELL: How Hot Is It?

Countless millions have gone along with Christianity merely as a form of "fire insurance."
  –Stephen Van Eck, Deism.com

"Go to Hell!"

Nearly everyone, at one time or another, has heard someone shout the above curse. Perhaps we have even used it ourselves. But how many of us consider what it really means? Based on traditional Christian belief, we are condemning the person who has offended us to a place of eternal punishment where "Satan" and his forces of evil are the caretakers.

What the Hell?

In Christian etymology, hell is known as the Lake of Fire (a *very* hot place) and is the destination for people whose names are not written in the "Book of Life" (Revelation 20:12). Many Christians believe it is a place of endless physical, mental, and emotional torture. In other words, if you end up there, you are going to suffer unspeakable agony, burning forever in a supernatural lake of fire.

Not a very pleasant thought – but then that's the whole idea.

A Hell of a Lot of People

According to the Bible, the people that are *excluded* from the Book of Life are "the cowardly, the faithless, the polluted, the murderers, the fornicators, the sorcerers, the idolaters, and all liars" (Revelation 21:8). The author of Matthew's gospel adds the "accursed" – those who refuse to take care of the hungry, thirsty, homeless, naked, sick and imprisoned (Matthew 25:41-46). Paul sums it up in 1 Corinthians 6:9 by simply stating the "wrongdoers" will be left out.

Conservative Christians do away with all these appellations and simply say the "unsaved" (non-Christians) are bound for hell. In other words, only those who have repented of their sins and accepted Jesus Christ as their personal savior will escape damnation.

During my later years in Christianity, this exclusive viewpoint became a sticking point for me. What about members of other religions (e.g., Buddhism, Hinduism, Judaism, Baha'i)? Or people who had never heard of Jesus? Of course I was provided with numerous scriptures that "supported" this ideology, but there was a part of me that simply could not accept the premise that people who were outside the Christian faith would, by default, be condemned to hell. One scripture that was never referenced is found in the gospel of Luke, where Jesus reportedly said: "Father, forgive them; for they know not what they do" (Luke 23:34 ASV). If people do not "know," how can they be condemned? Furthermore, there are millions who lived and died before Christianity ever came into being so how can they be accountable to its terms?

Christianity is said to be one of the world's largest religions (one-third of the earth's population[106]). However, based on the Christian salvation requirements, there are sure a "hell of a lot of people" that are not going to make it to "heaven." In fact, according to conservative Protestant criteria, perhaps 90% of people worldwide are headed for hell.[107]

Scare the Hell Out of ...

Although my conversion to Christianity was on a loving note (For God so loved the world ... John 3:16), it didn't take long to learn that hell was just around the corner if I didn't stay true to my faith. In addition, I was given the solemn charge to reach out to others so they too could avoid eternal fire and brimstone. And this directive was not given just once. My duty to evangelize "the lost" was repeated again and again in many and varied ways.

Whether it was personal witnessing or handing out tracts that described in vivid detail the fate of the unsaved, I did my best to fulfill my "sworn duty" as a born-again Christian. I put aside the misgivings I felt about encroaching on the lives of others and zealously gave the warning to repent or be bound for hell.

If you have ever been on the receiving end of this spontaneous preaching, you know how terribly irritating it is. However, what you probably don't realize is the impact the message has on your subconscious. Forcing you to consider your ultimate destiny can create a considerable amount of inner turmoil. Of course this is the whole idea behind evangelization efforts. Fear is a highly motivating factor. In fact, one source commented: "Fear of punishment in Hell, either for the believer or for unsaved friends and family of the believer, has probably caused more personal anxiety and distress than any other single Christian belief."[108]

As children we are threatened with the boogeyman when we disobey. As adults we are threatened with the horrors of hell.

A Hell of a Mess

During my research for this chapter, I discovered there are a myriad of doctrines related to hell, including when an individual actually arrives at this fearsome place. Believers back up their various views with scripture; however, as with all matters of faith, it boils down to interpretation and/or what they have been taught by church leaders.

As noted above, Christian traditionalists believe the "lake of fire" is a literal location and a place of everlasting punishment. (This view was promoted by Augustine, the early church father previously referenced, and later by Thomas Aquinas, 1225-1274

CE). However, whether the physical body and/or the soul/spirit suffers is problematic. Many in the Christian world believe that the soul separates from the body at death,[109] thus it is the *soul* that suffers (can the soul feel pain?). However, this view is complicated by the fact that Jesus was supposedly "seen" in *physical* form after his death. Paul attempted to explain all this in 1 Corinthians 15:44 where he writes there is both a physical body and a spiritual body and Jesus appeared in his "spiritual body." (Many of today's theologians teach Jesus was resurrected in a "reconstituted" body, whatever that is.) To complicate matters even further, some in the Christian world believe both the physical body *and* the soul will suffer.

Other Christians, who cannot accept the idea that God would torture unbelievers forever, believe in "Conditionalism" or "Conditional Immortality." This doctrine teaches the wicked suffer in in hell just long enough to pay for the nature and frequency of their sins while on earth and then they are annihilated (destroyed forever). They cite the scripture in 2 Thessalonians 1:9a where Paul writes: "These will suffer the punishment of eternal *destruction* ..." (i.e., termination, end, death).

Other believers alter this idea slightly and contend that after a time of punishment, because of God's love and mercy, all sinners will receive salvation.[110] The idea that a person would suffer eternally is seen as irrational and unjust. This teaching is known as Universal Reconciliation, or Universal Salvation, and is widely accepted among less conservative church-goers.

Many Christians say hell is separation from the presence of God (2 Thessalonians 1:9b), yet how can this be when God is said to be omnipresent? The psalmist David even asks the question: "Where can I go from your spirit? Or where can I flee from your presence?" (Psalm 139:7). To answer this question, some theologians say God *is* present in hell – for the sole purpose

CHAPTER 6. HELL: HOW HOT IS IT?

of dispensing divine punishment on the wicked. For those who believe in eternal punishment, I cannot help but ask, does this mean God is watching as unrepentant sinners suffer?

Many of the more secular or postmodern believers contend the "hellish" conditions expressed in the Bible are symbolic and should not be taken literally. To them, hell is a state of mind, not a place. Another belief says there is no divine retribution; everyone who leads a good life will go to heaven and enjoy eternity in the presence of God.

And finally, to some, hell is simply another word for death. There is no afterlife. There is no judgment. There is no punishment. We simply cease to be.

This last interpretation lines up with the early Hebrew Scriptures (Job 14:4 KJV; Ecclesiastes 9:5) where, although surprising to some, there is not one verse that speaks of endless punishment or an eternity of torture after one dies. Nothing in the Torah suggests anything, good or bad, will happen to an individual after death. In fact, it is only in Daniel's post-exilic writings that any mention is made about a return to life (and thus, some type of afterlife experience).

An interesting side note on the above paragraph – there is a scripture in Genesis where God tells the first couple they would surely *die* if they ate the fruit from the Tree of Knowledge (Genesis 2:17). When they chose to partake anyway, God placed certain curses on them during their lifetime and declared one day they would return to the dust from whence they came (Genesis 3:19). Nowhere does it say they would be forever tortured in fire and brimstone. Paul even writes in Romans 6:23 – "for the wages of sin is *death*" (not eternal life in hellfire). And Ezekiel (18:4 KJV) clearly states "the soul that sinneth, it shall *die*."

Arrival time is another contentious area. There are those who believe a person "arrives" at the moment of death, while others contend the wicked sleep until the resurrection, at which time they will be judged and condemned to the "lake of fire." Roman Catholics teach the doctrine of "purgatory," which means some people, depending on their past history, may have to wait a few years in a "temporary" hell before they get to move on to heaven.

Thus, we are left with several mutually inconclusive beliefs about hell. Only one, at most, can be true. Of course, no one knows which one that is, although Christians will cite numerous scriptures to validate the one they believe in.

Much more to the point is where did all these varied beliefs originate? With the doctrine of hell so embedded within Christian theology, I was intensely curious to know where and how it all started.

The Hell You Say!

Myths and legends about the afterlife destiny of human souls exist in countless cultures and religions, with some written nearly four thousand years ago.[111] All tell of a mysterious and shadowy place that lies beneath the ordinary world. It is known by various names, including the "Realm of the Dead," the "Land of No Return," the "House of Darkness," and the "Netherworld." In a Sumero-Akkadian myth (*The Descent of Ishtar to the Netherworld*), it is described as "the house which none leave who have entered it."

Some legends say that supernatural, otherworldly inhabitants, such as fairies, demons, giants, and monsters, dwell within the boundaries of this desolate place. To reach its depths, the deceased often must cross a bridge or river, or pass through a cave, well, or pit. It is nearly always said to be terrifying and dangerous, yet there is no mention of judgment or punishment in any of the earliest tales.

The Road to Hell

As discussed earlier, the early Hebrews saw the afterlife as a shadowy place known as *sheol* (grave, pit, abyss). All who died went there; there was no segregation between the righteous and the non-righteous. Over time, as the Jewish people faced death and destruction at the hands of their enemies, they began to visualize *sheol* as being divided into different areas with the most wicked (usually the foreign kings) being sent to the "depths of the Pit"(Isaiah 14:15, see also Ezekiel 32:23). However, there is no suggestion of postmortem punishment.

The ancient Egyptians, who believed in the immortality of the soul, were the first to teach afterlife judgment. The deceased were judged by Osiris, the Egyptian god of the underworld. Any soul he deemed evil underwent a "second death" and would experience either terrifying darkness or a river of fire. Some were devoured by a demonic crocodile. Good souls were allowed to enter the Blessed Land, an afterlife paradise.

The Persians (Zoroastrians) were another culture that believed in the survival of the soul. They agreed with the Egyptians on an afterlife judgment, but felt it would occur after the dead were resurrected (rather than in the underworld) when deceased souls would reunite with their bodies at the "last judgment." Those who were judged good would be allowed into paradise, a place of beauty, light, and pleasant scents. Those considered evil were sent to a place of unspeakable torment. (The actual teachings of Zoroaster, the founder of Zoroastrianism, are much more complex than what is stated here and readers are encouraged to explore this further. The similarities to Christian perspectives on hell and the afterlife are significant.)

The Greeks also taught that the soul lived on after death, but without any later reunion with the body. *Hades* was their realm for the dead and was ruled by a god of the same name. In older Greek myths, *hades* was a misty and gloomy underground abode that housed all who died. Later Greek philosophy introduced the idea that after death all souls were judged and either rewarded or cursed. If the latter, they were sent to *tartarus* (below *hades*) where they suffered eternal torment. (In the original text of the New Testament, the word *tartarus* is used in 2 Peter 2:4 where he claims it was the destination of the angels that sinned.)

We already know the Jewish people were greatly influenced by other cultures. After all, they lived among the Egyptians for four hundred plus years, among the Persians for a couple of centuries, and Greek thinking played a strong role from the fourth century BCE until well into the first centuries of the Common Era. Thus, it is not surprising their views on the afterlife changed. *Sheol* slowly lost its neutrality and death became a doorway to another life.

It was Paul, a Hellenistic Jew, who refined the Christian theology of the hereafter and accompanying judgment. In various epistles, he wrote: the dead are raised/resurrected with spiritual bodies (1 Corinthians 15:44); all who die "in Christ" will be changed (1 Corinthians 15:51); God will pass judgment and none will escape (Romans 2:3); the "good" will receive eternal life while the "evil" will receive wrath and fury … anguish and distress (Romans 2:7-9). (Note: he does not say the wrath, etc. will be eternal; nor does he mention anything about burning.)

It is important to note that Paul's epistles were circulated 10-20 years *before* any of the gospels were written. By the time the Jesus reporters developed their stories, Paul's teachings about the division between good and bad in the hereafter were solidly entrenched within the Christian community.

A Snowball's Chance in Hell

I could now see how the belief in afterlife judgment developed over the centuries, but what about the teaching that hell is a place of blazing fire and horrific torture? Where and how did this doctrine get started? My research revealed that, once again, the imaginative writers of the so-called "silent years," the post-exilic period of Jewish history, were the main culprits behind the flames of hell.

Burn, baby, burn

The Book of Enoch (discussed in a previous chapter) seems to be one of the primary sources. In fact, it is said to be one of the first apocalyptic books that associates fire with punishment.

As we know, "Enoch" wrote about the so-called fallen angels (the "Watchers") who mated with human women and produced offspring with them. For their crimes, they were punished by being led off to the "abyss of the fire: to the torment and the prison in which they shall be confined for ever."[112] Never again will they be able to ascend into heaven, but shall remain imprisoned inside the earth for all eternity.[113]

The book is also full of detailed accounts about several cosmic journeys that Enoch took. I was struck by the number of times he used the word "fire" to describe what he saw. For example, he said the ones who accompanied him were like flaming fire. He also mentions fiery bows and arrows, fiery swords, rivers of fire, heavenly fires, tongues of fire, portals of fire, streams of fire, mountains of fire, and of course, the abyss of fire that holds the naughty angels. In none of these scenes, however, is the word "hell" used.

It is an accepted belief within Christianity that "sinners" are the ones bound for hell. Although the writers of the Book of Enoch make frequent mention of "sinners," the closest reference I could find that might indicate an encounter with the "fires of hell" is at the very end of the book. It is in a section known as "Noah Fragments" and is thought to be extraneous to the original writings.

> *"And wait ye indeed till sin has passed away, for their names shall be blotted out of the book of life and out of the holy books, and their seed shall be destroyed for ever, and their spirits shall be slain, and they shall cry and make lamentation in a place that is a chaotic wilderness, and in the fire shall they burn; for there is no earth there. And I saw there something like an invisible cloud; for by reason of its depth I could not look over, and I saw a flame of fire blazing brightly, and things like shining mountains circling and sweeping to and fro. And I asked one of the holy angels who was with me and said unto him: 'What is this shining thing? for it is not a heaven but only the flame of a blazing fire, and the voice of weeping and crying and lamentation and strong pain.' And he said unto me: 'This place which thou seest-here are cast the spirits of sinners and blasphemers, and of those who work wickedness, and of those who pervert everything that the Lord hath spoken through the mouth of the prophets – (even) the things that shall be."* (1 Enoch 108:3-6)

At one time, the Book of Enoch was looked upon as Holy Scripture and many of the early church fathers (Tertullian,[114] Justin Martyr, Irenaeus, Origen, Clement of Alexandria) referred to it in their writings. For example, obviously referring to the passage quoted above, Justin Martyr (c. 100-165 CE) wrote in *First Apology 21*: "We believe that they who live wickedly and do not repent will be punished in everlasting fire." Other patristic writers used similar phrases to describe afterlife punishment.[115]

Enoch's book eventually fell out of favor and was *banned as heretical* at the Council of Laodicea in 365 CE. The question that comes to my mind is this: Is it possible that the entire doctrine of sinners weeping and crying as they endure the pains of a blazing flame is based upon one section of a book that was never given authoritative standing?

To varying degrees, the fires of hell are also addressed in several other Jewish pseudepigrapha. In *The Revelation of Moses*, God instructs the angel Gabriel to accompany Moses on a visit to hell. Moses balks at this and says, "I cannot enter Hell, that blazing fire," but God assures him he will be safe. As Moses enters hell, he sees some terrible things, such as sinners hanging by their eyelids, ears, tongues, and hands. Women are hanging by their hair and breasts. Men are hanging from their sexual organs. Others are hanging by their feet and their bodies are covered by black worms. Some have scorpions swarming all over them. All of them are crying out for an end to their pain, but they cannot die. When Moses questions the "Master of Hell" why the people are suffering such punishment, he is told of the sins they committed against God and the children of Israel.[116]

There are a few surviving fragments from the *Apocalypse of Zephaniah* that also include references to tormenting flames. Apparently, Zephaniah is taken to see the destiny of souls after death. There are three scenes, each introduced by trumpets sounded by angels (remind you of anything?). At the second trumpet, the heavens are opened and Zephaniah sees the sinful souls (which are given body and hair) tormented in a sea of flame.

One other citation I would like to mention is in the Apocrypha.[117] The book of Judith (most likely written in the late second century BCE) includes this verse: "The Lord, the Almighty, will punish them on the Day of Judgment by putting fire and worms into their flesh, so that they cry out with pain unto all eternity." (Judith 16:17)

Sounding the (Fire) Alarm

A very important point to keep in mind when considering these writings – all of these authors were *writing to the Jewish people*. They were warning them about what would happen if they didn't turn back to *Yahweh*. For example, in the *Revelation of Moses*, when Moses finally returns to God's presence, he makes this statement: "May it be Thy will, O Lord, my God, and God of my fathers, that Thou mayest save me and **Thy people Israel** from those places which I have seen in Hell" (emphasis added).

As mentioned elsewhere in this book, the essential mission of the apocalyptic writers was to reassure the people that God was in control, their enemies would eventually be destroyed, and Israel would one day return to its rightful place in the world. And, contrary to what is taught in many churches today, comments made by Jesus related to punishment (by fire or otherwise) were also directed to the Jews[118] (more on this below).

Hell? No!

Many Christians are familiar with scriptures in three of the gospels (Matthew, Mark, and Luke) where Jesus reportedly warned his listeners to avoid certain acts because of the danger of being judged and/or being cast into "hell" or "hell of fire." In the original text, the word the gospel writers used in each of these instances was *gehenna*, which is from the Greek word, *geenna* and is the equivalent of the Hebrew *ge-hinnon*, which literally means the "valley of Hinnom."

Historically, the valley of Hinnom[119] is where King Ahaz made molten images to the pagan god Moloch and then performed the abominable practice of burning his own sons for a sacrifice (2 Chronicles 28:3 NIV; Jeremiah 19:4-5 NIV). The Bible reports that King Manasseh did the same (2 Chronicles 33:1, 6 NIV). Eventually Josiah, a righteous king, abolished these reprehensible practices. In later years, the area became known as the Valley of the Slaughter (Jeremiah 7:31-32) – a burial place for the corpses of those who did evil in God's sight.

From my research, it seems the idea of a burning *gehenna* was first advanced during the twelfth century CE by Rabbi David Kimhi. In his commentary on Psalms 27:13, he wrote:

> *"Gehenna is a repugnant place, into which filth and cadavers are thrown, and in which fires perpetually burn in order to consume the filth and bones; on which account, by analogy, the judgment of the wicked is called 'Gehenna.'"*[120]

In 1926, two German theologians, Hermann Strack and Paul Billerbeck, wrote a commentary in which they disagreed with Rabbi Kimhi. They stated they were unable to find any archeological or literary evidence in earlier intertestamental writings or later rabbinic sources to support the Rabbi's claim.[121] Several other scholars concur.[122]

Nevertheless, based on numerous publications and commentaries over the years, it is apparent many theologians do agree with the Rabbi and are convinced *gehenna* was a smoldering rubbish heap and therefore, a fitting metaphor for "hell."

When we look at the scriptures without prejudice, it is clear a horrible sacrilege took place in the valley of Hinnom, and God exacted a severe punishment on the perpetrators. As time passed, the Jews began to see *gehenna* as a symbol of the consequences of sin, but never as a place of torment beyond death. This view did not come until long after Jesus had died.

Isaiah's Outdoor Incinerator

From my personal experience, I knew that many in the church believe a scripture found in Isaiah 66:24 offers proof that the valley served as an outdoor incinerator (even though *gehenna* is not mentioned):

> *And they shall go out and look at the dead bodies of the people who have rebelled against me; for their worm shall not die, their fire shall not be quenched...*

However, when taken in context, Thayer[123] believes the prophet was describing judgment against the enemies of Israel and offering comfort to the captives in Babylon. Most believers reject this viewpoint and are certain Isaiah is providing an accurate description of *gehenna*. Some even go so far as to say this scripture is describing what will happen after the Final Judgment; i.e., the "saints" will be able to view the wicked writhing in torment. This latter idea probably comes from the Book of Enoch, where it is written: "Here they will be gathered together and here will be their place of judgment. In the last days there will be upon them the spectacle of righteous judgment in the presence of the righteous forever." (1 Enoch 27:3)

In addition to its long-standing reputation as a burning garbage heap, I discovered there are several other myths related to *gehenna*: God created it as a place of punishment *before* Creation; its fires began to burn on the first Sabbath; it is half fire, half hail; there are seven thousand scorpions within its crevices; it is ruled by a prince; etc.[124]

Get the Hell Out

In the original text of scripture, the word "hell" is nowhere to be found. Yet in the King James Version (KJV) of the Bible, the word is used 54 times! In nearly every instance, it is used as a replacement for the Hebrew word *sheol* (Old Testament) or the Greek word *hades* (New Testament), both of which mean nothing more than the grave, a dark unknown state, the abode of the dead (not the abode of the wicked). A good example can be found in the Book of Acts where the KJV reads: "Because thou wilt not leave my soul in hell" (Acts 2:27). The original word here is *hades*.

Strangely, *hades* is translated correctly as "grave" in 1 Corinthians 15:55: "O grave *[hades]*, where is thy victory?" Yet in Revelations 20:14, it reads "death and hell *[hades]* were cast into the lake of fire." (I've often wondered how "hell" could be cast into the Lake of Fire if, according to some Christian beliefs, they are one and the same.)

From the previous discussion, we already know that *gehenna* and "hell" are one and the same in many Bible translations.

In 2 Peter 2:4, we find the word "hell" again, but in this case, it is a translation of the Greek word *tartarus* (the place where the fallen angels will reside until "the judgment").

As I continued to probe this subject, the question came to mind: How did the word "hell" come to be used in the first place? Why didn't the KJV translators simply use the word grave? With a little extra digging, I learned an interesting fact about the word "hell." It is actually derived from the Old English word *hel, helle* and came into being around 725 CE as a reference to the netherworld of the dead. Its core meaning is "to hide, conceal." Perhaps the KJV translators felt this word was more utilitarian as it encompassed the meaning of both *sheol* and *hades*.

One thing is clear. Its meaning evolved over the years. Where it was once used to describe the dark and dismal abode of departed spirits, in today's idiom it has come to mean the place of eternal punishment for the wicked.[125] (Curious thought: if the word *sheol* truly means fire and punishment, as it is often translated, why would Job, 14:13, ask to go there?)

Does Death Do Us Part?

The idea of endless torture in a never-ending (is that even possible?) fire is directly connected to the belief in an immortal soul; meaning, at death the soul leaves the body and lives on consciously forever. As already discussed, this teaching began with the Egyptians and was later adopted by the Greeks (and popularized by Plato). Eventually, it was accepted as "truth" among the Hellenistic Christian communities, even though the doctrine itself is not biblical.[126]

Jeffrey B. Russell, history and religious studies professor,[127] believes the reason the idea took hold is because the early Christian theologians admired Greek philosophy and found support there for the immortal soul.[128] We already know the writings of Tertullian, Justin, and Augustine indicate their belief in the soul's immortality.[129] In subsequent years, influenced by these Nicene and Post-Nicene authors, Protestant reformers Martin Luther and John Calvin, et al, furthered the idea of the immortal soul. And in 1513, the Roman Catholic Church fully incorporated the teaching into its articles of Christian belief.

In today's world, many evangelical preachers carry on this erroneous teaching. For example, Dr. Billy Graham writes in Chapter 6 of his book Peace with God (1984), "The Bible teaches that you are an immortal soul. Your soul is eternal and will live forever." He goes on to say, "The Bible teaches that whether we are saved or lost, there is conscious and everlasting existence of the soul and personality."[130]

The Fire That Refuses To Die

One of the reasons an ever-burning hell has remained imbedded within Christian thought is due to the creation of the Latin Vulgate by the Catholic Church. This version of the Bible "reigned supreme for over a thousand years and the doctrine of hell became deeply entrenched into the psyche of the Christian world as a true biblical doctrine."[131] Since the KJV has been the standard Bible for Protestant Christianity for nearly 350 years, it is not surprising that the ongoing belief in an eternal hell has remained intact.

Final Thoughts

In a pluralistic, post-modern world, it is difficult to understand why people continue to believe in hell – in whatever form they visualize it. Or that preachers, pastors, and priests continue to propagate a doctrine rooted in myths and legends formed long before Christianity was born.

Of course, I cannot deny that I followed suit during my years within the Christian environment. If it came from the pulpit, then it must be true. It has taken years of research, along with an open and curious mind, to overcome the doctrines that I accepted without question. I find it sad that so many of today's churches prefer to picture God as a bloodthirsty monster who maintains an everlasting Auschwitz for his enemies,[132] rather than a God who loves, who forgives, and whose greatest desire is to have a relationship with humankind.

Jesus came to share a message of God's love and mercy. The few occasions where he is said to mention "hell" were to warn an unrepentant people that God was not happy with their disobedience and unfaithfulness. Nowhere did he refer to it as being a place of everlasting torment for those who didn't swear allegiance to him.

Life is not an ordeal during which the soul struggles to get to heaven and avoid hell. Rather life is an ongoing process by which the soul seeks to know God. Why do we spend our time on earth always keeping an eye towards what awaits us in the afterlife? NOW is the only time there is.

7. END TIMES: Famines, Earthquakes, Wars ... Oh My!

"If the apocalypse comes, beep me."
  –Buffy, the Vampire Slayer

People have been obsessed with how the world will end for generations. Multiple individuals have advanced multiple scenarios about what might happen in the last days. Some accounts are so outrageous the average person just shakes their head in disbelief. Others have a hint of potentiality (think colliding asteroids or other cosmic disasters).

As I write this, December 21, 2012 is fast approaching and thousands believe a catastrophe of immense proportions will occur on this date. In fact, some fear the earth will be destroyed. The belief is based on stories surrounding an ancient Mayan calendar, which doomsayers are certain predicts such an apocalypse. However, when the facts are thoroughly investigated, there is little evidence that anything calamitous will occur.[133]

The Christian world has its own end-time scenario. It involves the rise of an "Antichrist," a horrific period of tribulation, a final battle between "Satan" and Christ, a city that floats down out of the sky, and the establishment of a utopian world. The faithful believe all of this is outlined in the book of Revelation (also referred to as the Apocalypse of John), which is the final entry of the New Testament (a fitting placement).

An Enigmatic Discourse

For most people, the book of Revelation is extremely puzzling and difficult to follow (many have never even read it). Its contents are mysterious, confusing, bizarre and for many, intensely frightening.[134] It is laden with cryptic images and spine-chilling events. The author, a Jewish-Christian who identifies himself as "John," writes of poisoned waters, rivers of blood, and hail made of fire. He tells of locusts with scorpion-like stingers that are allowed to torture unbelievers for five months. He warns of famines, wars, earthquakes, and other disasters. He describes horses with lions' heads and tails like serpents. He also includes a story about a beast with seven heads and ten horns that rises up from the sea. The beast resembles a leopard, but has feet like a bear and a mouth like a lion.

To interpret the contents of this book literally is to stretch human imagination to the extreme. Yet there are scores of theologians, past and present, who have attempted to do just that by giving contemporary meaning to the phantasmagoria of words, numbers, colors, images, and phenomena contained within its pages. And millions of Christians use these renderings to visualize the future of the world.

A Common Oversight

While the larger content of John's work is inscrutable, he makes a very clear statement at the beginning of his discourse. He writes in Revelation 1:1 that what God gave him to share "must **soon** take place" (emphasis added). The word *soon* is generally defined as being in the near future, shortly, or before long.

Two thousand years have passed since John wrote these words, yet believers are certain the described events are congruent to their own era. In fact, during the Middle Ages "the sure and urgent expectation of the end-time was, quite literally, a fact of life."[135] Even today, Christians read the Bible and the newspaper simultaneously and see *The End* just around the corner.

But does this unrelenting expectation have merit? Was John really prophesizing the end of the world? Is an "Antichrist" truly destined to appear in the Last Days to rule the world? (See

Chapter 8.) And will a celestial warrior-king miraculously appear in the clouds one day to reward the faithful?

What's It All About, Alfie?[136]

John wrote his book from an apocalyptic perspective. As discussed elsewhere, this type of writing was very common in the two centuries before and after the birth of Christ. Born out of great turmoil, persecution, and oppression, the authors told stories of how God would one day bring an end to history and begin again with a new world. Nearly always the narratives were the result of visions, dreams, and visits by supernatural messengers. Unearthly images and highly symbolic language were part and parcel of these other-worldly tales.

While modern readers often turn to Christian leaders for interpretation and explanation of John's obscure writings, this was not the case for people living in the ancient world. They were well-acquainted with the complex nature of apocalyptic literature. For them, the strange characters, images, symbols, and events were immediately intelligible. In other words, they *knew* what John was writing about. They understood he was railing against the Romans for their treatment of the first century church.

Under Attack

The inhabitants of Rome viewed Christian worship practices as alien and highly distasteful. They saw the "love feasts" as immoral, thought that calling each other "brother" or "sister" was incestuous, and considered the ritual of eating Christ's flesh as cannibalism. Thus was created a strong atmosphere of distrust and suspicion, even hate, which resulted in many Christians being arrested and killed.

Conditions became unbearable under the reign (64-68 CE) of the emperor Nero, who was well-known (and feared) as a Christian-hater. According to the Roman historian Tacitus, believers were forced to serve as objects of amusement and frequently inflicted with great cruelties. Some were torn to death by dogs, others crucified, and many were set on fire to serve as nighttime illumination.[137] Fortunately, Nero's persecution was short-lived, but even after his reign it was considered a capital crime to be a Christian.

Some years later (81 CE), the Roman Emperor Domitian[138] ascended the throne. He reigned until 96 CE and is considered to be one of the most savage and wicked rulers in the first century.[139] He claimed to be a god and made it his personal mission to brutally massacre all who professed to be a Christ follower. Hundreds upon hundreds were marched into the Roman Coliseum and killed by the swords and spears of the gladiators.

Retribution

Yes, there was no doubt in the minds of Revelation's early readers – John was sorely grieved at what was happening to the Christians and desperately wanted the harshest punishment possible to be inflicted on this terrible regime. It is apparent he was driven by anger as he envisioned a gathering of the kings of the whole world (remember the size of John's world) for a great battle against God the Almighty (Revelation 16:14). In his mind's eye, he saw much spilled blood and lots of earth-shaking (literally). But for John, the outcome of this brutal conflict was certain. The heavens would open and an unidentified rider[140] on a white horse (Revelation 19:11-13, 16) would appear, accompanied by a host of angels to "strike down the nations" (Revelation 19:15).

In true apocalyptic style, John finishes his discourse by describing a "new heaven and a new earth" (Revelation 21:1)

CHAPTER 7. END TIMES: FAMINES, EARTHQUAKES, WARS, OH MY!

Still Waiting

When John's predictions (the fall of Rome and return of Jesus) did not occur within the next few decades, Christian leaders began their attempts to "futurize" John's message. These efforts continue to this day. As a result, the majority of Christians believe this final book of the Bible is an end-time prophecy that describes a chilling view of humanity's future. Few believe, or even *want* to believe, that John's statements of imminence were intended for first century readers, not for Christians of today. In fact, many point to passages in the New Testament and assert that even Jesus predicted the end-of-the world. But did he? Or have his words been flavored by teachings that arose several decades after his death?

The Words of Jesus

Jesus left no written record so we have no way of knowing what he really said during his time on this earth. We can only rely on gospels written several decades after his death by individuals who saw him as the long-awaited Messiah, believed he had been resurrected, and awaited his return to set up God's kingdom. That's why it's so important to place Jesus at the appropriate moment in history as we consider his words. This means acknowledging that he was speaking to the Hebrew people – *not* to Christians because at that point in time (Jesus' lifetime), there was no such animal.

The End of the World or the End of the Age?

In the beginning of Chapter 24 of Matthew,[141] the author tells us that Jesus walked out of the temple and told his disciples that "not one stone will be left here upon another; all will be thrown down." A little while later, he is sitting on the Mount of Olives and the disciples ask him when all of this will take place. What will be the signs? Jesus then goes into a lengthy account of events that he expects to happen.

According to many in the Christian world, Jesus is giving his listeners a prophecy about earth's final days. This idea seems to be based upon the translation in the King James Version of the Bible[142] which suggests that the disciples asked "... what shall be the sign of thy coming, and of the end of the *world?*"

According to original Greek manuscripts, the word Jesus actually uses in this passage is *aion*, which means "age or period of time" (the Greek word for "world" is *kosmos)*. The Jewish people considered the time before the Messiah as one age (Mosaic Age) and the time after the advent of the Messiah to be another age (Messianic Age). Thus, they were asking Jesus about the Messianic Age or the "age to come." They wanted to know when the Kingdom of God[143] would finally be established.

The Warnings

The gospel writers tell us that Jesus immediately warned them not to be led astray by false prophets and messiahs (remember, the Jewish people had been waiting centuries for the *mashiach* to appear), and cautioned them not to believe any signs or wonders these pretenders might perform. He told them they would most likely experience various hardships before their final deliverance, but it was important for them to stay faithful and be ready for the end of days (*aharit ha-yamim*). Most importantly, he made it clear that no one would know exactly when any of this would take place.

As previously mentioned, this portion of scripture has long been used by Christians to maintain that Jesus was prophesying about the end of the world. However, when we remove the persona placed on him by these first century writers, it becomes clear he was speaking to his own people about the long-awaited restoration of their nation.

The Time Has Come ... and Gone

Probably because of its mystifying contents, the book of Revelation seems to have a strange effect on people. One writer commented that it serves as a "stimulant that fills them with frantic energy"[144] and they find themselves compelled to *do* something to move things along. Over the years, this frenetic anticipation has driven numerous men and women to devote a large part of their lives trying to pinpoint when that Big Moment will arrive so they and others can be prepared.

Even though Jesus (Mark 13:32), along with Paul (1 Thessalonians 5:2), and John (Revelation 3:3), warned that God's kingdom would arrive without forewarning, this has not deterred would-be oracles from setting a date for the end of days.

The Celestial Stopwatch

Around 90 CE, Saint Clement 1 predicted the world's end would occur at any moment. In 365 CE, a man by the name of Hilary of Poitiers announced the end would happen that year. Saint Martin of Tours, a student of Hilary, was convinced the end would happen sometime before 400 CE.

Many Christians in Europe predicted the Big Event would occur on January 1, 1000. Some even gave their possessions to the Church in anticipation of The End. Others believed it would occur in 1033, the 1000th anniversary of the death and resurrection of Jesus. Pope Innocent III added 666 years onto the date that Islam was founded and thereby became convinced The Big Day would occur in 1284.

The list goes on and on.

In more recent times, William Miller (1782-1849) was certain the Great Day would take place sometime between March 21, 1843 and March 21, 1844. When the time passed and nothing happened, it was said to be a "calculation error" and the true date should have been October 22, 1844. Once again, the Great Day never came to pass and thus it became the Great Disappointment.

One of Miller's followers, a woman named Ellen White[145] (1827-1915), said she had experienced a number of "divine visions" that convinced her Miller was all wrong. She predicted certain events had to occur first and once they took place, the Big Day would arrive. She firmly believed it would occur during her own lifetime but unfortunately, the world failed to "end on time."

Mormon Joseph Smith (1805-1844) reported he was praying one day and a voice told him the "Son of Man" would not return until he (Joseph) was eighty-five years old. He died at age thirty-nine, long before the projected date arrived. Another prophesy gone down the tube.

The Jehovah's Witnesses (Watchtower Bible and Tract Society) said the "battle of the Great Day of God Almighty" was to occur in 1914. They based this prophecy on the book of Daniel, Chapter 4, using their own interpretation of the "times" that Daniel wrote about. Of course, 1914 came and went and nothing happened. They then reset the date to 1925, which was, according to their Watchtower magazine, "a date definitely and clearly marked in the Scriptures." One more prophesy unfilled.

Even though none of these end-time predictions have come to pass, it has not discouraged others from adding their voice – with one significant difference. Modern-day prophets have learned not to attach a date or time to their forecasting. Instead they reference the state of the world and warn that certain portentous milestones signal the final curtain is ready to fall.

As an example, some viewed the First World War as a "sign of Christ's coming." In 1945, thoughts of the apocalypse took a quantum leap forward with the detonation of the first atomic bomb. To many in the fundamentalist movement, the 1948 granting of statehood to Israel was another sure sign that things were winding down. Former President Ronald Reagan saw the 1971 coup in Libya as a definite signal that end-time events were falling into place.[146]

Hal Lindsey, a contemporary writer, became one of the most famous seers in modern history as he warned of the imminent end of the world in his book, *The Late Great Planet Earth* (1970). Carefully he spelled out the procession of events (sans dates) so Christians would know what to watch for and thus be fully prepared for the Momentous Occasion. (For many years, I clung to Lindsey's predictions ... watching and waiting for the signs of the end-times.)

A couple decades later (1995), Tim LaHaye and Jerry B. Jenkins delivered their slick *Left Behind* series, in which they used fiction to spell out the future battle between God and "Satan" and its final conclusion.

Final Thoughts

For many years I believed what the church told me about John's Revelation. There was no doubt in my mind that Jesus was going to return in the clouds of heaven to collect the saints (the "Rapture"[147]), then do battle with the "beast," the "false prophet," and the "kings of the earth" at a place called Armageddon (Hebrew: *Har-Magedon*).[148] He would, of course, be triumphant.

I held onto the fervent hope that I would see the "new Jerusalem" floating down from heaven (Revelation 21:2), drink of the water of life, walk the streets of gold, and live happily ever after in God's presence.

However, as I studied the scriptures, it became clear to me that the Book of Revelation is related to a particular time in history, to a particular set of circumstances, and to a particular people. It is not, as I was taught, a prophecy of things to come.

The world may very well end someday, but probably not in our lifetime. According to science, the earth has a good five billion years before the warranty on our sun runs out. I find this prophecy far more realistic than the nebulous signs, omens, portents, and numbers that Christians believe point to a more immediate ending.

Not long back, I came across a saying that pretty much sums up my feelings about the end times: "Don't worry about the world coming to an end today. It's already tomorrow in Australia."[149]

ADDENDUM: In 2011, while I was writing this book, a pastor in Oakland, CA predicted the end of the world would occur on May 21, 2011. The day came and went without anything happening. The Bible provides an apt description of such actions: *For the wisdom of this world is foolishness to God. As the Scriptures say, "He traps the wise in the snare of their own cleverness"* (1 Corinthians 3:19, NLT).

8. ANTICHRIST: The Master Deceiver

"We are never deceived; we deceive ourselves."
　–Johann Wolfgang von Goethe

"Clouds that thunder do not always rain."
　–Armenian proverb

Within the Christian scenario of the final days is a figure known as the Antichrist. It is believed by many that he is an actual human being who will one day become the leader of a nefarious worldwide empire. He will advance his cause surreptitiously and only the "elect" will recognize the wickedness behind his actions. Eventually he will face Jesus in an epic battle for the faithful.

As part of the evangelical community, I was taught to ever be on the lookout for this evil-minded antagonist. I was repeatedly warned that his rise to fame and power were imminent considering the state of the world. Since I am no longer a Christian, I suppose I will now be among the deceived and thus fall under the imposter's sinister power.

Hidden Identity

The appearance of the Antichrist has long been associated with the book of Revelation, yet nowhere does the author mention a personage by that name.[150] Nevertheless, virtually all modern-day evangelicals are certain this is who John is writing about when he mentions the Beast, the Dragon, the False Prophet, and the Whore of Babylon. Some theologians argue as well that Paul's reference to the "lawless one" in 2 Thessalonians is the Antichrist,[151] and others say Daniel was referring to the Antichrist when he wrote about the "little horn" in chapter 7. As with many other Christian teachings, various Bible passages are cited to create the desired effect.

Probably the portion of scripture that is most relied upon to bolster the cause of an Antichrist is found in the first and second epistle of John[152] where he mentions the *antichrist* (not capitalized). However, a close read of 1 John 2:22 makes it clear the author is writing about those in the Jewish community who deny that "Jesus is the Christ" (i.e., God's anointed one, the *mashiach*). This includes anyone who does not acknowledge that Jesus came in the flesh. He explains it more fully in 1 John 4:1-3 NIV (emphasis added):

> *Dear friends, do not believe every spirit, but test the spirits to see whether they are from God, because many false prophets have gone out into the world. This is how you can recognize the Spirit of God: Every spirit that acknowledges that Jesus Christ has come in the flesh is from God, but every spirit that does not acknowledge Jesus is not from God.* ***This is the spirit of the antichrist****, which you have heard is coming and **even now is already in the world**.*

Again, he writes in 2 John 1:7 NIV (emphasis added):

> *Many deceivers, who do not acknowledge Jesus Christ as coming in the flesh, have gone out into the world.* ***Any such person*** *is the deceiver and the **antichrist**.*

In other words, any person who denied Jesus came in the flesh possessed the spirit of the antichrist. He also warned (1 John 2:28) that many of these "false prophets" were circulating among the people and promoting their ideas. He was especially concerned because he believed these "antichrists" were a signal of the "last hour" (before the anticipated return of Jesus).[153]

There is no indication that John was pointing to one particular individual as the celestial embodiment of evil. In fact, one scholar commented that John would probably be stunned to learn his use of the word had come to symbolize the ultimate enemy of the Church.

First Sightings

The key questions then become: Where did the concept of an in-the-flesh Antichrist originate? And how did it become central to the way the story of Revelation is interpreted in later centuries, all the way down to the present?

The first seeds of the idea probably came from the apocalyptic literature (First Enoch is a good example), in which a cosmic conflict between God and some evil force would take place at the end of days. These imaginative writers interpreted every event on earth "as part of a cosmic drama designed and orchestrated by beings who exist in a transcendental reality."[154]

Further, stories about a mythological dragon opposing a creative deity had been circulating among many cultures for several centuries, so it is not surprising that the author of Revelation would write about a "beast" and a "dragon."

The Transmutation

My research indicates the transmutation from 1 John's *spirit of the antichrist* into the *"Antichrist"* originated near the beginning of the second century. This was a time of great persecution, hatred, and brutal treatment of the early Christians by tyrannical Roman emperors. As each ruler seemed to become more brutal than the one before, it wasn't long before the "evil force" referenced by the apocalyptic writers and the "spirit of antichrist" metamorphosed into a full-fledged human being, manipulated and directed by "Satan" himself.

The Changing Paradigm

Early church fathers helped things along as they "interpreted" texts and documents according to their own personal understanding. Even though their writings and dissertations were nothing more than opinion and speculation, much of what they claimed set precedents for centuries to come.

In fact, popular Christian preaching throughout the early Middle Ages repeated and reinforced their ideas until they became part and parcel of today's Christian teachings.

One of the earliest to attach the devil's personality to 1 John's *antichrist* is Polycarp of Smyrna (c. 69-155 CE) where he wrote (emphasis added):

> "Everyone who does not confess that Jesus Christ has come in the flesh is an antichrist; whoever does not confess the testimony of the cross is **of the devil**; and whoever perverts the sayings of the Lord for his own desires, and says that there is neither resurrection nor judgment, such a one is the **firstborn of Satan**."[155]

Two other major sources for the antichrist myth tradition were Irenaeus and Hippolytus.[156] In 189 CE, Ireneus agrees with and expands on Polycarp's thoughts when he writes in *Against Heresies* (emphasis added):

> "[B]y means of the events which shall occur in the time of the Antichrist it is shown that he, being an apostate and a robber, is anxious to be adored as God, and that although a mere slave, he wishes to be proclaimed as king. For he, being endued with all the **power of the devil**, shall not come as a righteous king nor as a legitimate king in subjection to God, but as an impious, unjust, and **lawless one** ..."

Shortly thereafter, Hippolytus (around 200 CE) set the tradition that there would be one Antichrist as there was one Christ, and that Antichrist would "ape and imitate Christ in every possible way in order to deceive us."[157] In an account about the Final Enemy, he outlines the six ways in which the Antichrist will be a perverted imitation of Christ: (1) Jewish origin; (2) the sending out of apostles; (3) bringing together people scattered abroad; (4) sealing of his followers; (5) appearance in the form of a man; and (6) the building of a temple in Jerusalem."[158] He insists the Antichrist is the son of the devil and the vessel of Satan.

Cyril of Jerusalem (315-386 CE), a distinguished theologian of the early church, wrote: "Antichrist will exceed in malice, perversity, lust, wickedness, impiety, and ruthlessness and barbarity all men that have ever disgraced human nature. Hence St. Paul emphatically calls him 'the man of sin the son of perdition, the wicked one, whose birth and coming is through the operation of Satan, in all manner of seduction and iniquity.'"[159]

During the 8th century, a monk named John of Damascus wrote: "Everyone who does not confess that the Son of God is God come in flesh ... is antichrist. Nevertheless, in a peculiar and special way is that one called Antichrist who comes at the consummation of the age."[160]

Sometime around 950 CE, the permutation was moved along by a monk named Adso of Montier-En-Der, who wrote a treatise on the Antichrist. It was Adso's claim that the Antichrist would be born from the union of a father and mother (not from a sole virgin) and conceived wholly in sin because the devil would enter the mother's womb at the moment of conception. Throughout his life, evil spirits would be his constant companions. He would also have access to magicians, enchanters, diviners, and wizards who, at the devil's bidding, would instruct him in every evil way. At the end of time, he would torture the people of God for three and a half years and then be killed through the power of Jesus.[161]

The Power of Words

It is clear these writers profoundly influenced the development of the Antichrist myth. Indeed, their comments formed the building blocks from which the modern figure of Antichrist emerged. Yet, they are not scripture. They are simply the words of creative human beings who believed they had the inside scoop on God's plan.

Even so, many Christians today agree with all or part of their writings and are certain the Antichrist is a human being who will appear on the world's scene in the last days. He will be controlled by none other than the Big Bad Guy and his goal will be to deceive, ensnare, and destroy. It is said his life and rise to power will imitate, mimic, closely resemble, or counterfeit Jesus' own path.

The Passing Parade

As with the drive to figure out when the world will end, so too has there been scores of pseudo-prophets trying to identify or name the individual they believe will fill the role of Antichrist.

In the early days of Christianity, along with Caligula, the emperor Nero was also seen as the Antichrist. Subsequent centuries have witnessed a parade of candidates, including Charlemagne King of the Holy Roman Empire; Napoleon Bonaparte; Benito Mussolini; Adolf Hitler; and in recent times, Henry Kissinger; Mikhail Gorbachev; Pope John Paul II; Saddam Hussein; Vladimir Putin; King Juan Carlos of Spain; Karl Von Habsburg of the Habsburg Dynasty; Javier Solana of the European Union; Prince Charles of Wales -- and more recently and controversially, Barack Obama, President of the United States.

While not naming names, some modern-day believers unequivocally state the Antichrist will emerge as the leader of a European "super-state" (aka the Revived Roman Empire), which will arise out of the current European Union. They say he will arrange a peace settlement for Israel and her neighbors, establish a worldwide economic network, set up the "abomination of desolation"[162] (i.e., an image of himself in the rebuilt Jewish Temple), and finally be assassinated. But that's not the end of this evildoer. He will then be resurrected, win the Nobel Peace Prize, and be named Time's Man of the Year. After these triumphs, he will set himself up as God to rule the world.

The Antichrist Craze

Hollywood, never one to let an opportunity slip by, has capitalized greatly on the Antichrist legend. Many reading this may recall *Rosemary's Baby* and *The Omen* series, along with *The Devil's Advocate*, *End of Days*, and *The Seventh Sign*. *The Omega Code* is a more recent film that portrays the Antichrist as a European leader. *Alien 4, Resurrection* appears to be an allegory on the birth of Christ with interspersed Antichrist themes. Such films have even given non-Christians pause as to the possibility of evil personified.

Not to be left out, several authors have written about the Antichrist. Stephen King has intertwined hints of the Antichrist in several of his books (e.g., *The Stand*, *Eyes of the Dragon*, the *Dark Tower* series). Other books include *The Coming Prince*, *The Age of the Antichrist*, the *Left Behind* series, and *The Mark of the Beast*. One rather strange book, published in 1979, maintained that the Antichrist is monitoring everyone even now through our television sets.[163]

Final Thoughts

The fascination with the eventual end of the world choreographed by a powerful "Satan-like" figure continues to thrive in the lives of both Christians and non-Christians. Events and personalities are scrutinized using the Bible, the shifting currents of popular culture, and portentous acts of nature in an effort to determine how close we are to John's so-called divine prophesies described in Revelation.

Rather than focus on a fearsome figurehead that threatens from the future to destroy the Church, how much more fruitful would it be to focus on *today* and follow the advice of Micah (6:8) "... to do justice, and to love kindness, and to walk humbly with your God"?

John F. Kennedy once said: "The great enemy of the truth is very often not the lie, deliberate, contrived and dishonest, but the myth, persistent, persuasive and unrealistic."

9. GOD: The X Factor

"Concepts about God and traditions about God are not God."
–Gary Amirault

In the Western world, whenever anyone speaks of "God," they nearly always are referring to the Judeo-Christian God, a "Super Being" (male) with transcendental powers that created and rules the universe. This entity is believed to exist "up there" (witness the number of people who look skyward when referring to God) or "out there," beyond the heavens, somewhere in the universe, separate from the world "He" made. Some see Him as being seated on a throne, clothed in snow white, with hair like pure wool (Daniel 7:9).

Others have noted that God dwells in a burning bush, between the cherubim, among the people of Israel, in a tabernacle, inside a temple, and even within church walls ("God's house"). Some even feel He resides in religious objects (e.g., statues, images, crucifixes). Paul told the Corinthians that God lives within (1 Corinthians 3:16).

Many consider Him to be the Big Judge in the sky who watches every move we make, hears every word we speak, and knows every thought we have. In addition, He is seen as the Supreme Commander who has total control over a person's eternal destiny.

Yet, with all this phenomenal power, people feel they can relate to this entity in a personal way, similar to a good friend. He is considered analogous to human beings in that He can speak, breathe, see, hear, walk and talk, as well as portray other human attributes, such as anger, jealousy, love, compassion, forgiveness, etc. William Lane Craig (Christian apologist) puts it this way: God is "endowed with rationality, self-consciousness, and volition."[164] A sect of Christians in the fourth century even believed God had a human form.[165] The early church fathers dismissed it almost contemptuously, considering it to be extreme ignorance. Most of today's Christians would agree – yet Jesus is said to be God and he had a human body.[166]

Christians feel their God should be consulted on every aspect of their lives since He is all-knowing (omniscient). They also believe Him to be all-powerful with total control over everything that happens both to them and in the world (omnipotent). And even though He is often viewed as being somewhere "out there," they believe Him to be everywhere at once (omnipresent).

Many of the faithful feel that without God, there is no purpose to life. He is their center of being, i.e., the basis for their existence. Without Him, they would have no one to turn to in time of crisis. They would be without guidance when making major decisions in life. Some even feel that they would have no moral guidelines. Most of all, without God they believe they would lose their ticket to an afterlife filled with good and happy things.

The X-Factor

With all that God means to Christians, when you ask them to describe their God, few have a ready answer. They may tell you what God means to them personally, they may quote scriptures about God, or they may use the aforementioned adjectives (omnipotent, omniscient, omnipresent) – but to actually put into words who or what God is seems to be a near impossible task. Some have gone so far as to say it is impossible for the finite mind of humans to define God. Perhaps part of the problem is that within Christianity there are actually *three* Gods, although believers will argue the three are simply different aspects of *one* God (more on this later).

Interestingly, non-Christians seem to be able to answer the question quite readily. One person I asked said God is an all-loving, all-powerful being who created everything there is. Another gave a more esoteric description by saying that God means "existence." And someone defined God as the Truth that is unfathomable. An online website provided the very abstract definition of God as the "Transcendental Signifier."

One individual supplied me with this profound definition: "A massive energy source that can transfer its energy, storing it into living things and allowing us to use it to function and transfer that energy into new beings as well. (Energy cannot be created or destroyed. So the energy we have in us was transferred from a previously existing energy source, not simply created.)"

Paul Tillich, a Christian existentialist philosopher, used the term "Ground of Being" to describe God. In his opinion, humans need something to overcome our existential angst, i.e., our fear of death.[167] We need something "out there" to save us, to help us overcome the dread of our demise. To Tillich, God is this "Ground of Being," the agent that helps us deal with our finitude.

An online dictionary defines God this way: "A being of supernatural powers or attributes, believed in and worshiped by a people, especially a male deity thought to control some part of nature or reality."

A few other definitions I came across are: God is love, God is nature, God is the infinite potentiality that underlies all matter and energy, God is the force behind the creation of the universe and the laws of nature.

My personal definition is that God is *Universal Presence* – but even that falls short of how I see God.

Atheists (and secular humanists) often define God as nothing more than superstition, but more often they ask the question: "Can a thing which does not exist be defined?"

The basic truth is this: People may say they believe in God, but most have no clear idea exactly who or what that "God" is. One person summed it up by asking God this question: "Do any of us actually know what you are all about? We worship, revere, and pray to you but have absolutely no clue about you – who you are, where you came from, why you are, where you are, what you are … or if you even exist."

Part of the mystery may be due to the fact that throughout history God has had many forms.

In The Beginning, Gods

While the prevailing belief within Christianity is that a singular deity created the heaven and the earth (*In the beginning, God created the heaven and the earth.* Genesis 1:1 KJV), there are many who disagree with this solo god concept. Several Eastern religions, as well as a number of tribal religions in Africa and the Americas, worship or believe in more than one god (polytheism). In fact, according to historians and archeologists, men and women throughout the ages have offered worship to literally thousands of gods and goddesses.

Way Back When

No one knows for certain when religion first appeared on the scene, but nearly every scholar believes it was in response to human fear. The early humans lived in an unpredictable and often capricious environment over which they had no control. They did not understand the constant changing of seasons; the movement of the sun, moon, and stars; the storms, dry spells, floods, earthquakes, etc. And what they did not understand, they feared.

As a way to help explain the world around them, the early hunter-gatherers created gods. One god controlled the wind. Another had control over the rain and thunder. Others were in charge of the rivers, the rocks, the trees. They even believed the sun was a god.[168] Scholars call this *primal religion,* best defined by its inter-relationship with nature, animals, and objects both animate and inanimate.

One of the core reasons for creating gods was to gain a sense of security in the face of natural forces.[169] It helped these primitive people to know that "something" was at work behind the scenes. While the presumed belief has been that the primitives feared their gods, one source[170] suggests they saw them as good and believed the world would always be as the gods had made it. In many ways, this same idea holds true today, i.e., the world is the way it is (entirely or in part) because a supernatural being is in control.

Since woman is generally considered to be the source of life, many contend the early gods were females (goddesses). Mesopotamia, said to be the "cradle of civilization," worshiped a female god known as *Ishtar,* and some readers may be familiar with *Isis,* a goddess of ancient Egypt. According to Professor Kunal Chakrabarti, who teaches history of religion at the Jawaharlal Nehru University in New Delhi, India, "All primitive religions from the earliest Neolithic period were based on goddesses. There was no concept of god because the goddess symbolized the feminine principle of fecundity, and man's role in the creative process was not understood."[171] In an article written shortly before her death, Marija Gimbutas, UCLA professor of archaeology, concluded: "The focus of life for these peoples [ancient civilizations] was religion: the perpetual functioning of the cycle of life, death, and regeneration [was] embodied by a central feminine force – the Goddess."[172]

The actual transformation from female to male deities is debated, but some feel it came with the discovery and spread of written language. Others believe it was related to the nomadic Indo-Europeans who invaded the early farming communities, bringing with them their fierce warrior gods and eventually wiping out the reign of the goddess.[173]

As cultures evolved, the duties of the deities became more sophisticated. Now they were responsible for everything – from controlling the weather to making bread and pottery to enhancing fertility. At some point, creator gods came into being, along with stories of how each of these gods (or goddesses) "created" the world.[174] In time, the various gods were organized into a cosmic family (pantheon), with each one serving a particular purpose.

In the early Assyro-Babylonian religion, deities became identified with heavenly bodies; i.e., the sun, moon, planets, and stars, and were given names. Each god was assigned a "seat" in the heavens and certain "traits" were attributed to each one. One was portrayed as full of mercy and kindness; another was the protector of mankind; while the chief trait of *Shamash*, the Sun-God, was justice.

Over the years, gods have been in the form of animals, a combination of human and animal, and finally by the time of the Greeks, gods (and goddesses) were totally in human form. In addition, many cultures (e.g., Greek, Roman, Norse, Native Americans, etc.) anthropomorphized their gods; that is, they ascribed to them not only human form, but also human attributes (feelings, moods). Many of these gods were said to interact with each other, as well as with humans. Some even believed their gods had minds remarkably similar to humans.

Hundreds of major gods are recorded in world history and many are still recognized throughout the world.[175] Nearly all of them are seen as supernatural beings that must be worshipped.

Altars, elaborate statues, and temples are often built to honor them, and religious leaders (known by many names) perform rituals and sacrifices in hopes of influencing the various deities.

And Then There Was One

Somewhere along the way, monotheism (belief in a single, all-powerful god) entered the picture. According to the New World Encyclopedia website,[176] monotheism is often seen as the "ideal" concept of god and is said to be the most "civilized" view of divinity. Monotheists tend to see their god as the creator of the world who oversees and intervenes in human events and is the source of the highest good. They believe their god is superior to all other gods ("My god is better than your god") and even go so far as to deny the existence of gods belonging to other religions.

Scholars are unsure of monotheism's exact origin, but some suggest it first arose in Zoroastrianism (*Ahura Mazda*), considered to be one of the world's earliest religions. Others have argued that Egypt was the birthplace when, during the fourteenth century BCE, the Pharaoh Akhenaten declared *Aten* (aka *Aton*) to be Egypt's only god. The worship of all other gods was forbidden and this solar god became known as the "king of the gods."[177]

Disregarding scholarly input, most Bible believers would emphatically state that Judaism is the original monotheistic religion – even though the Old Testament is full of stories that show the people of Israel were primarily polytheists.[178] (There is considerable biblical and anthropological evidence that also supports this.)

The Bible tells of one individual (Abraham) who tried early on to sell the people on the idea of one god, but for the most part he was unsuccessful. Several years later another fellow (Moses) did his best to promote monotheism – he even delivered a message direct from the Big Guy (*I am the Lord your God ... you shall have no other gods before me*, Exodus 20:2-3), but it didn't seem to change anything. The Jewish people continued to build altars and perform sacrifices to gods such as Baal, Marduk, Molech, Dagon, Chemost, Milcom, and others.[179]

Several biblical scholars are convinced the transition to monotheism did not actually occur until the sixth century BCE when the Israelites were taken into captivity by the Babylonians. The reign of the idolatrous kings ended and the priests (who were generally monotheistic) assumed leadership. After the Persians conquered Babylonia, they fortified the idea by teaching the Jews about Zoroastrianism. In the end, the belief in a singular deity prevailed.

Even though it took several centuries for the idea of a solo god to take a firm hold among the Jewish people, once it did they became fiercely monotheistic. They now see *Yahweh* as the one who created the universe and is above all earthly things ... an eternal, all-powerful being that is beyond human limits of comprehension.

Mystical Math

Most consider Christianity, the adopted child of Judaism, to also be a monotheistic faith. However, some feel this is a misnomer because of the "Trinity" doctrine. According to this teaching, God is divided into three separate entities. There is God the Father, God the Son (Jesus), and God the Holy Spirit. The belief is that each is distinct yet coexists as one being.

This threefold view of God was one of the most confusing aspects of the Christian faith for me. Almost from the beginning, I wrestled with it – and was puzzled when there seemed to be no ready answer. The only response I ever got from church leaders was that it was a "mystery."[180] Finally, in order to move on in my religious experience, I resolved the issue by telling myself that, in any given situation, each member of the trio would think and act the same.

Once I left Christianity, it seemed prudent to learn more about this doctrine ... and what I discovered may surprise some readers. **The doctrine of the trinity was *not* taught by the early Christians, nor is the word found anywhere in the Bible**.[181]

It was not until the late second century, when Theophilus of Antioch wrote his *Apology to Autolycus*, that the word was actually used. What I found intriguing is his use of the word was different than what most recognize (Father, Son, and Holy Spirit). To Theophilus, the "trinity" (Greek: *trias*) meant "God, his Word, and his Wisdom."[182]

It wasn't until the early third century that Tertullian, a Latin theologian, wrote a treatise in which he definitively described the trinity as including the Father, Son, and Spirit. Over the next several years, church fathers (Hippolytus of Rome, Origen, Novatian) began to include and expand on the theology. Finally, Gregory (c. 213–c. 270), a bishop in Asia Minor, wrote a *Declaration of Faith* which treated the Trinity as standard theological vocabulary. About a century later, in 325, the First Council of Nicaea established the doctrine as orthodoxy and made it a part of the Nicene Creed.[183] It is also spelled out in the Anathasian Creed,[184] which was completed sometime in the fifth century.

It is interesting to note that the gods of many ancient religions also came in threes. For example, the Babylonians had Anu, Bel, and Ena; the Egyptians had Osiris, Horus, and Isis; and the Romans had Jupiter, Pluto, and Neptune. In today's world, Hinduism, the main religion of India, recognizes the trinity of Brahma, Vishnu, and Shiva. Christian theologians will deny any similarity, saying these gods are separate entities and not "joined" into one substance as in the Trinity.[185]

Despite its widespread acceptance among Christians, the Trinity doctrine has been a stumbling block to non-Christians throughout its history. The intensely monotheistic Jews completely reject the concept because it denies the "oneness" of *Yahweh*, which they believe is unmistakably taught in the Hebrew Scriptures.

The Need for God(s)

Whether God is one or many, people have turned to supernaturalism for centuries. A hypothesis has even been proposed that a "God gene" (more accurately called a "faith gene") is hardwired into the DNA of humans that predisposes them towards spiritual or mystic experiences. A far more likely scenario is that humans feel a need for the numinous due to their fear of the unknown, particularly as it relates to their mortality. By depending on some magical unseen force, they are able to face an uncertain world and, for some, look forward to a paradisal afterlife.[186]

From Devout to Doubt

For several years, I joined millions of others and looked to the Christian God for spiritual sustenance. I prayed to, worshipped, and praised "Him." He was my helpmate, a shelter in the storm, and the One who would someday walk with me through the valley of the shadow of death. I believed He had total control over what happened to me, good or bad, so when things went favorably, I offered gratitude. When things turned out unfavorably, I "justified" the results by telling myself it was "God's will." I strived to always "do the right thing" because if I didn't, I feared I might end up in a very bad place that didn't include this God. As a result, my "godly" feelings often alternated between fear and love.

Prior to my "conversion" my religious life had been virtually non-existent so I totally relied on my pastor, church leaders, and other believers to show me how to live a "holy life." In problematic circumstances, they were also the ones I turned to for advice and counseling. I never questioned the validity of anything I was told; I simply accepted and believed. As a result, I began to assimilate their beliefs, ideas, and thinking. No surprise that *my* image of God soon matched *their* image of God.

I was enthusiastic about my faith. I felt privileged that I was in an elite group of people who had God on their side. I believed everything that came from the pulpit and absorbed Bible scripture like a sponge. I eagerly awaited each opportunity to be back in church with like-minded people. In my mind, there was absolutely no doubt that Jesus had given his life so the world could be saved ... and I shared this belief every chance I got. Most of all, I looked forward to spending eternity with God the Father and Jesus the Son.

I also enjoyed being able to use God as my personal "genie in a bottle" whenever I wanted or needed something. My requests were sometimes as mundane as asking for a promotion, the signal lights to all be green when I was rushed, or my kids to behave when we had company. On other occasions, my petitions were more serious, like coping with the death of a loved one, healing for myself or a friend, dealing with some kind of disaster, or simply asking God to intervene in a crisis.

On the more ordinary issues, I was naturally disappointed if God didn't respond, but on critical, sometimes life-threatening matters, I had a difficult time understanding why God hadn't moved on my behalf. Especially when the Bible says in Matthew 7:7, "Ask and it will be given you ..." and in Matthew 21:22 (NKJV), "And whatever things you ask in prayer, believing, you will receive." Even Luke (11:10) writes, "For everyone who asks receives ..." As might be expected, church leaders always seemed to have a myriad of reasons why prayers sometimes go unanswered, although I often felt many of them sounded more like rationalizations than bona fide explanations.

Nevertheless, God was a vital part of my life for a number of years and I was completely and utterly convinced He existed and had great things in store for me.

Second Thoughts

As time went on, however, several things happened that gave me pause; each one intrinsically entwined with the Christian concept of God that I had once so enthusiastically embraced.

At first, I noticed a number of comments from the pulpit seemed to lack plausibility. While I continued to receive the words with respect and reverence (after all, a "man of God" was saying these things), questions began to form in my mind. I experienced similar reservations when reading the Bible. Numerous discrepancies I had previously overlooked now stood out. The fantastical stories about Moses and the Red Sea, Noah and the flood, Jonah and the whale, Joshua and the walls of Jericho, and (most of all) the resurrection of Jesus, became harder and harder to swallow. I began to question the existence of the entity called "Satan" and his unholy rule over "hell." Still, it never occurred to me to consider them as anything but "truth."

Before long, other doubts and uncertainties surfaced and I could feel the authenticity of my Christian experience dwindling away. My long-held faith in the Christian God was crumbling. Even though a part of me was afraid to *not* believe (because of the "consequences"), the light of reality and reason began to overcome the shadows of apprehension and fear. Eventually, I knew it was time to travel a different pathway.

Emerging from Darkness

I freely admit I struggled as I walked away from a life that had, at one time, been all-consuming. Even though I knew in my heart of hearts that my decision was the right one, the warnings against "backsliding"[187] reverberated in my subconscious for a very long time. It took extensive reading and research – and introspection – before I was able to erase the harsh and unforgiving doctrines of the church.

Then one day, almost as an epiphany, I noticed I was no longer afraid, worried, or scared. The fear that I might do something to offend God and thus be condemned to the fires of "hell" had disappeared. My heart was at ease. The darkness had lifted.

It was in that moment that I *knew*, within the deepest part of my being, that my concept of spirituality – and of "God" – had changed. Dramatically.

Seeing God in a New Way

Quite frankly, for me to now use the word "god" is difficult. It carries too much baggage and does not represent how I view the marvelous and amazing force that exists all around me. I have found the description that works best for me is *Universal Presence*, but even these words do not encompass the awe and inspiration that stirs within me when I gaze up at the stars at night. My mind staggers as I contemplate the billions and billions of galaxies and try to understand how it all came to be and why I am a part of it.

One thing is certain. I simply cannot attribute it to some mystical supernatural being that is said to exist somewhere "out there." No, it is not the work of some god; it is the manifestation of a power that cannot be defined.

How can we possibly put a "face" on something that is infinite and uncreated? How can we conceptualize an entity that is not limited by dimensions in any way? Any "god" we might create is inadequate and falls far short of the essence exhibited in our wondrous cosmos.

For me, this magnificent Presence encompasses all time and space and is everywhere and in every now. It is within every tiny molecule, every atomic particle. It exists within you and within me. It is the mystery of our beingness.

In my mind, we dare not ... we cannot ... put a name on that which exists simply because it is.

Final Thoughts

For too many years, I listened to what others told me about God and spent far too little time examining my own heart and beliefs. It took a long while to untangle the messages that had settled deep within my cells. Only through much soul-searching and listening to my inner voice did I finally discover the Absolute that exists beyond all that we can ever know or comprehend. This pure and loving energy is now a vital and integral part of my being.

Do I know why I am here or what will happen when my time on this earth is done? No, but it matters not because I have learned to accept life as being neither more nor less than it is. I've stopped worrying about what tomorrow holds. Instead I focus on the present, the "now" ... because that is really all we have. To spend my days fretting about an "afterlife" takes away from the contentment that fills every part of my being.

Realizing that I am merely a speck of dust in the grand scheme of things, I never cease to express my gratitude for the opportunity I have been given to live on this planet ... in this solar system ... in this galaxy ... in this universe ... at this moment in space and time.

In closing, consider this question that a five-year-old might ask: "Where did the world come from?" If you tell him that God made it, he will very likely ask, "Then where did God come from?" What will be your answer?

EPILOGUE

Do you remember playing "Follow the Leader" when you were a kid? Wherever the "leader" went, you followed. Down the street, across the vacant lot, through rain puddles, under low hanging branches ... it didn't matter. You just laughed and followed along. Sometimes the leader would do crazy things, like hopscotch along the sidewalk, "fly" like an airplane, or walk like a drunken sailor. Naturally, you were expected to follow along.

And you did.

As adults, many of us continue to "follow the leader." This is not always a bad thing because there are times when we definitely need guidance and direction in order to live harmoniously among other humans. But we have to be careful. It can be too easy to lose our way in the process. And when this happens, we may unwittingly allow the "leaders" to do our thinking for us.

This is especially true when it comes to spiritual matters.

Most readers have heard or read about the Jim Jones tragedy, the David Koresh fiasco, and the Heaven's Gate suicides. These are prime examples of what happens when we do not exercise our own powers of reason. Yes, these are extreme cases, but anyone who follows a religious leader without question is susceptible.

To Know is More Than to Believe

One of my main goals for this book has been to encourage Christians to *know* what they believe and why. As I learned from my own experience, it is far too easy to "follow the leader" and simply accept what you are taught in church and Sunday School as the "Christian Story" when, in fact, there is an abundance of information that is never presented.

Even the Bible cannot be considered the final resource as it is only evidence in and of itself. Moreover, as I have pointed out, the authors were writing about the cultures, events, and people of their time. Trying to integrate present-day persuasions into its pages frequently misconstrues the meaning and message the writers sought to convey.

It is not my desire to convert the religious. I'm just asking you to examine what you believe ... to look outside the box, beyond long-held convictions. Be willing to open your heart and mind to new information. I won't deny that by doing so, you may run the risk of dismantling cherished beliefs.

But if, just if, you find truth in what I have shared with you in this book, then I will have fulfilled my goal of helping you enjoy a more loving relationship with your God – one that is free from guilt and fear.

May you always live a life that is authentically yours.

RESOURCES

Books

Benammi (pseud.): *Aspects of Jewish Life and Thought (Letters of Benammi)* (NY, Bernard G. Richards Co., 1922)

Benson, Andrew D.: *The Origins of Christianity and the Bible: An Historical and Archeological Approach* (CA, Prudential Publishing Co, 1997)

Bernstein, Alan E.: *The Formation of Hell: Death and Retribution in the Ancient and Early Christian Worlds* (NY, Cornell University Press, 1993)

Bettenson, Henry and Maunder, Chris, eds., *Documents of the Christian Church, 3rd ed.* (USA, Oxford University Press, 1999)

Borg, Marcus: *Jesus: Apocalyptic Prophet of the New Millennium* (USA, Oxford University Press, 1999)

_____*Meeting Jesus Again for the First Time* (NY, HarperCollins, 1994)

_____*Reading the Bible Again for the First Time* (NY: HarperCollins, 2001)

_____*The God We Never Knew: Beyond Dogmatic Religion to a More Authentic Contemporary Faith* (HarperSanFrancisco, 1997)

Boyce, Mary. *Zoroastrians: Their Religious Beliefs and Practices* (London, Routledge, 1979, 2001)

Bütz, Jeffrey J.: *The Brother of Jesus and the Lost Teachings of Christianity* (VT, Inner Traditions, 2005)

Carr, David M: *An Introduction to the Bible* (UK, Wiley-Blackwell, 2010)

Cayce, Peter: *What Did Jesus Really Say – How Christianity Went Astray* (NY, iUniverse, 2005)

Charles, Louis: *Jesus Religion: A Critical Examination of Christian Insanity* (Angels and Ghosts, LLC, 2008)

Charlesworth, James H., editor: *The Old Testament Pseudepigrapha, Vol. One, Apocalyptic Literature and Testaments* (MA, Hendrickson Publishers, 1983)

Cohn, Norman, *Cosmos, Chaos and The World to Come* (New Haven and London, Yale University Press, 1993)

Crossan, John Dominic: *The Birth of Christianity: Discovering What Happened in the Years Immediately After the Execution of Jesus* (HarperSanFrancisco, 1998)

Ehrman, Bart D.: *Jesus, Interrupted; Revealing the Hidden Contradictions in the Bible (*and Why We Don't Know About Them) (NY, HarperCollins, 2009)

_____*Lost Scriptures: Books that Did Not Make It into the New Testament* (NY, Oxford University Press, 2003)

_____*Misquoting Jesus: The Story Behind Who Changed the Bible and Why* (NY, Harper Collins, 2005)

Elkins, David N.: *Beyond Religion: A Personal Program for Building a Spiritual Life Outside the Walls of Traditional Religion*: (IL, The Theosophical Publishing House, 1998)

Ellwood, Robert S. and Partin, Harry B.: *Religious and Spiritual Groups in Modern America, Second Edition* (NJ, Prentice Hall, 1998)

Enns, Paul: *Moody Handbook of Theology* (Chicago, Moody Press, 1989)

Evans, Craig A.: *Noncanonical Writings and New Testament Interpretation*, (Hendrickson Publishers, 1992)

Fox, Matthew: *Original Blessing: A Primer in Creation Spirituality* (NM, Bear & Co. Publishing, 1983)

Fredriksen, Paula: *From Jesus to Christ* (Yale University, 1988)

Freke, Timothy and Gandy, Peter. *The Jesus Mysteries: Was the "Original Jesus" a Pagan God?* (NY, Three Rivers Press, 1999)

Friedman, R.E: *Who Wrote the Bible?* (San Francisco, Harper Collins, 1997)

Fuller, Robert: *Naming the Antichrist: The History of an American Obsession* (Oxford University Press, 1995)

The Jesus Seminar: *The Five Gospels: The Search for the Authentic Words of Jesus* (NY, Macmillan Publishing, Polebridge Press, 1993)

Hopfe, Lewis M.: *Religions of the World, 4th Edition* (NY, MacMillan, 1987)

Jenks, Gregory Charles: *The Origins & Early Development of the Antichrist Myth*, (Walter de Gruyter, 1991)

Kelly, Henry Ansgar, *Satan: A Biography* (NY, Cambridge University Press, 2006)

Kirsch, Jonathan: *A History of the End of the World* (NY, HarperCollins, 2006)

Komarnitsky, Kris D.: *Doubting Jesus' Resurrection: What Happened in the Black Box?* (UT, Stone Arrow Books, 2009)

Laughlin, Paul Alan: *Remedial Christianity: What Every Believer Should Know about the Faith, but Probably Doesn't* (Santa Rosa, CA, Polebridge Press, 2000)

Maccoby, Hyam: *The Mythmaker: Paul and the Invention of Christianity* (NY, Harper & Row, 1986)

McGinn, Bernard: *The Antichrist: Two Thousand Years of the Human Fascination with Evil* (NY, Columbia University Press, 2000)

Mitchell, Stephen: *The Gospel According to Jesus: A New Translation and Guide to His Essential Teachings for Believers and Unbelievers* (NY, HarperCollins, 1991)

Pagels, Elaine: *The Origin of Satan: How Christians Demonized Jews, Pagans, and Heretics* (NY, Random House, 1995)

Paine, Thomas: *The Age of Reason* (NY, Dover Publications, 2004)

Pinnock, C.L, contributor: *"Four Views of Hell: The Conditional View,"* editor, William Crockett (Grand Rapids, Zondervan, 1992)

Russell, Jeffrey Burton: *The Devil: Perceptions of Evil from Antiquity to Primitive Christianity* (NY, Cornell University Press, 1977)

_____ *Satan: The Early Christian tradition*, (Cornell University Press, 1987)

Sanders, E.P: *The Historical Figure of Jesus* (London, Penguin Books, 1995)

Saranam, Sankara: *God Without Religion: Questioning Centuries of Accepted Truths* (GA, The Pranayama Institute, Inc., 2005)

Schwartz, Howard: *Tree of Souls: The Mythology of Judaism* (NY, Oxford University Press, 2004)

Segal, Alan F.: *Paul the Convert* (New Haven and London, Yale University Press, 1990)

Sheehan, Thomas: *The First Coming: How the Kingdom of God Became Christianity* (NY, Random House, 1986)

Spong, John Shelby: *Eternal Life: A New Vision* (NY, HarperOne, 2009)

_____*Rescuing the Bible from Fundamentalism: A Bishop Rethinks the Meaning of Scripture* (NY, Harper Collins, 1991)

Taylor, John Hammond (Translator and Annotator), *Ancient Christian Writings: St. Augustine, The Literal Meaning of Genesis, Vol. 2* (Paulist Press, 1982)

Thayer, Thomas B.: *The Origin and History of the Doctrine of Endless Punishment* (Boston, Universalist Publishing House, 1881)

Toynbee, Arnold, editor: *The Crucible of Christianity: Judaism, Hellenism and the Historical Background to the Christian Faith* (NY, World Publishing Company, 1969)

Turner, Alice K.: *The History of Hell* (Florida, Harcourt, Inc., 1993)

Vermes, Geza: *The Religion of Jesus the Jew* (MN, First Fortress Press, 1993)

Wilson, Barrie PhD.: *How Jesus Became Christian* (NY, St. Martin's Press, 2008)

Wray, T.J. and Mobley, Gregory: *The Birth of Satan: Tracing the Devil's Biblical Roots* (NY, Palgrave Macmillan, 2005)

Wylen, Stephen M. *The Jews in the Time of Jesus* (NJ, Paulist Press, 1996)

Websites

http://www.30ce.com
http://www.adherents.com
http://www.ancient-hebrew.org
http://www.ancienthistory.about.com
http://www.assemblyoftrueisrael.com
http://bbhchurchconnection.wordpress.com
http://www.blog.bibleplaces.com
http://www.churches.kconline.org
http://www.concordant.org
http://www.deism.com

http://www.earlychristianwritings.com
http://www.fsmitha.com
http://www.godchecker.com
http://www.godsplanforall.com
http://www.hell-on-line.org
http://www.hinduwebsite.com
http://iath.virginia.edu
http://www.iranvision.com
http://www.jesuspolice.com
http://www.kencollins.com
http://www.lifepositive.com
http://www.lostgoddesses.com
http://www.mb-soft.com
http://www.myjewishlearning.com
http://www.newadvent.org
http://news.nationalgeographic.com
http://www.newworldencyclopedia.org
http://www.patheos.com
http://www.pbs.org
http://www.pleaseconvinceme.com
http://www.religionnews.com
http://www.religion-online.org
http://www.religioustolerance.org
http://www.sacred-texts.com
http://www.sullivan-county.com
http://www.ucg.org
http://www.unitypublishing.com
http://en.wikipedia.org

Documentaries

After Jesus: The First Christians (CNN Presents)
Angels: Good or Evil (History)
Banned from the Bible (History)
From Jesus to Christ: The First Christians (PBS)
Gates of Hell (History)
God in America (PBS)
Who Was Jesus (Discovery)
Who Wrote the Bible (History)

APPENDIX

Estimated Range of Dates for Bible Books (Oldest to Newest)

Old Testament (BCE)

—Before Exile

Job	Varies from 2nd century to 6th century
Genesis	1450-1410
Exodus	1450-1410
Numbers	1450-1410
Leviticus	1445-1444
Psalms	1440-586
Deuteronomy	1407-1406
Joshua	1405-1383
Judges	1086-1004
Ruth	1046-1035
Song of Solomon	970-930
Proverbs	970-930
Ecclesiastes	935
1 and 2 Samuel	930's
Obadiah	853-841 or 605-586 (difficult to date)
Joel	841-835
Jonah	785-760
Amos	760-750
Micah	742-686
Hosea	715
Isaiah	700-681
Nahum	663-612
Zephaniah	630
Jeremiah	626-586 (includes Lamentations
Habakkuk	612-589

—After Exile

Ezekiel	571
1 and 2 Kings	560-538
Daniel	530
Haggai	520
Zechariah	520-480

Esther	470
Ezra	440
Nehemiah	430
1 and 2 Chronicles	430
Malachi	430

New Testament (CE)

1 Thessalonians	50-60
1 Corinthians	50-60
2 Corinthians	50-60
Galatians	50-60
Romans	50-60
Philippians	50-60
Philemon	50-60
Colossians	50-80
Hebrews	50-95
Mark	65-80
James	70-100
Ephesians	80-100
Matthew	80-100
2 Thessalonians	80-100 (Disputed as being written by Paul
1 Peter	80-110
Acts	80-130
Luke	80-130
Revelation	90-95
John	90-120
Jude	90-120
1, 2, 3 John	90-120
Titus	100-150
1 and 2 Timothy	100-150
2 Peter	100-160

SELECTED READING

Asimov, Isaac: *In the Beginning: Science Faces God in the Book of Genesis* (NY, The Stonesong Press, LLC, 1981)

Daniels, Kenneth W.: *Why I Believed: Reflections of a Former Missionary* (TX. Kenneth W. Daniels, 2009)

Davis, Craig: *Dating the Old Testament* (NY, RJ Communications, 2007)

Leedom, Tim C., editor: *The Book Your Church Doesn't Want You to Read* (CA, Truth Seeker Co., 2003)

Maziarek, Jeff: *Spirituality Simplified* (IL, SpiritSimple Enterprises, LLC, 2002)

Price, Robert M.: *Jesus is Dead* (American Atheist Press, 2007)

Segal, Alan F.: *Life After Death: A History of the Afterlife in the Religions of the West* (NY, Doubleday, 2004)

Templeton, Charles: *Farewell to God* (McClelland & Stewart, Toronto, Canada, 1996)

Tolle, Eckhart: *The Power of Now: A Guide to Spiritual Enlightenment* (CA, New World Library, 1999)

Walsch, Neale Donald: *Conversations with God: An Uncommon Dialogue, Book 1* (NY, G.P. Putnam's Sons, 1992)

_____ *What God Wants: A Compelling Answer to Humanity's Biggest Question* (NY, Atria Books, 2005)

Williamson, Marianne: *A Return to Love: Reflections on the Principles of A Course in Miracles* (NY, HarperCollins, 1992)

Wright, Robert: *The Evolution of God* (NY, Little, Brown and Company, 2009)

ENDNOTES

PREFACE

[1] David N. Elkins, *Beyond Religion: A Personal Program for Building a Spiritual Life Outside the Walls of Traditional Religion*: (Illinois, The Theosophical Publishing House, 1998) p.252

CHAPTER ONE

[2] "Dissecting Christianity's Mind-Snaring System" <http://www.deism.com/christianhype.htm>

[3] Marcus Borg, *Reading the Bible Again for the First Time* (NY, HarperCollins, 2001) p.11

[4] John Dominic Crossan, *The Birth of Christianity* (California, HarperSanFrancisco, 1998), p.54.

[5] Internet article: "Gilgamesh, Epic of" <http://www.newworldencyclopedia.org/entry/Gilgamesh,_Epic_of>

[6] Internet source: "Cuneiform Script" <http://en.wikipedia.org/wiki/Cuneiform_script>

[7] Bart D. Ehrman, *Misquoting Jesus: The Story Behind Who Changed the Bible and Why* (NY, Harper Collins, 2005), p.90

[8] Internet article: "Translating the Bible," see "The Actual Form of the Bible Text at that time" <mb-soft.com/believe/txh/version7.htm>

[9] *Misquoting Jesus*, p.55

[10] Paul Alan Laughlin, *Remedial Christianity: What Every Believer Should Know about the Faith, but Probably Doesn't* (Santa Rose, CA, Polebrige Press, 2000), p.12.

[11] Fragments have been found of several gospels, allegedly written by Mary Magdalene, Peter, and Judas. An entire manuscript was found in 1945 of the Coptic Gospel of Thomas.

(12) See "Early Christian Writings" for the most complete collection of documents from the first two centuries. <http://www.earlychristianwritings.com>

(13) *Misquoting Jesus*, p.152-153

(14) There are no original gospel documents. The earliest extant copies date to the fourth century and none of these 5,400 manuscripts are the same. It is estimated that the number of variations between manuscripts totals between 200,000 and 300,000.

(15) Interestingly, even though most of these writings were considered heretical, many of the precepts are part of modern Christian belief.

(16) Internet article: "About Those 'Literal' Translations" <http://kencollins.com/bible/bible-t4.htm>

(17) Most scholars believe Jesus spoke Aramaic.

(18) 14 books written during the intertestamental period that some believe have questionable value.

(19) Stephen M. Wylen, *The Jews in the Time of Jesus* (NJ, Paulist Press, 1996), p.40

(20) R.E. Friedman, *Who Wrote the Bible?* (San Francisco, Harper Collins, 1997)

(21) John Shelby Spong, *Rescuing the Bible from Fundamentalism* (NY, Harper Collins, 1991), p.33

(22) *Reading the Bible Again for the First Time*, p.28

(23) *The Jews in the Time of Jesus*, p.123

(24) *Reading the Bible Again for the First Time*, p.299

CHAPTER TWO

(25) *Meeting Jesus Again for the First Time* (NY, HarperCollins, 1994)

(26) Jesus, speaking Aramaic, could never have designated himself as the "son of man" in a Messianic sense because the Aramaic term never implied this meaning. (Source: JewishEncyclopedia.com)

(27) Scholars say the first gospel (attributed to Mark) was written c.70 CE, a full generation after Jesus' reported ministry.

(28) E.P. Sanders, *The Historical Figure of Jesus*, (London, Penguin Books, 1995); Bart Ehrman, *Jesus: Apocalyptic Prophet of the New Millennium* (USA, Oxford University Press, 1999); David M. Carr, *An Introduction to the Bible* (UK, Wiley-Blackwell, 2010); Laughlin, *Remedial Christianity*; et al

(29) Porphyry (234-c.305 CE) wrote in *Against the Christians 2* that the evangelists were "fiction-writers."

(30) According to Ehrman (*Misquoting Jesus*, 2005), there was an extraordinarily wide range of literature being produced, disseminated, read, and followed by early Christians.

(31) *The Historical Figure of Jesus*

(32) Internet article, "The Founder of Christianity by C.H. Dodd" <http://www.religion-online.org/showchapter.asp?title=2241&C=2109>

(33) A Jewish spiritual leader qualified to expound and apply Jewish law.

(34) Geza Vermes, *The Religion of Jesus the Jew* (MN, First Fortress Press, 1993), p.5

(35) Thomas Sheehan, *The First Coming: How the Kingdom of God Became Christianity* (NY, Random House 1986), p.35

(36) *The Jews in the Time of Jesus*, p. 23

(37) *The Jews in the Time of Jesus*, p. 49

(38) Prophets of devastation or ultimate doom.

(39) *The First Coming*, p.39

(40) "Zoroastrianism is the oldest of the revealed world-religions, and it has probably had more influence on mankind, directly and indirectly, than any other single faith," Mary Boyce, "*Zoroastrians: Their Religious Beliefs and Practices*," (Routledge, London, 1979, 2001), Introduction

(41) Internet article: "Zoroastrianism" <http://www.patheos.com/library/zoroastrianism.html>

(42) Lewis M. Hopfe, *Religions of the World*, 4th ed. (NY, MacMillan, 1987), p.259-283; see also Internet article, "The Battle Between Good and Evil in Zoroastrianism" <http://www.hinduwebsite.com/zoroastrianism/ahirman.asp>

(43) Some Christians may point to the writings of Daniel (12:2) as an indication that the Jewish people believed in resurrection and an afterlife. However, biblical scholars agree this book was penned during the reign of Antiochus and is part of the apocalyptic writings. There is no other reference to an afterlife in Hebrew scripture.

(44) The ancient Hebrews believed that upon death, people went to sheol, a Hebrew word for "grave" or "pit" that was located in a bleak subterranean region and was a place of dust, darkness, silence, and forgetfulness.

(45) A person who speaks for God. In the Old Testament, God used prophets to guide the people of Israel.

(46) Interpreting baptism as a sign of faith in Christ was a doctrine that came about much later. This was not its original purpose.

(47) The Hebrew word for kingdom is *malkut*, the Greek counterpart is *basileia*. Both terms mean "rule" or "reign."

CHAPTER THREE

(48) According to the New Revised Standard Version (1989) of the bible, ancient authorities mark the last twelve verses of Mark (16:9-20) as "doubtful." The current consensus among bible scholars is that they were not part of the original text. The New International Version (1984) concludes the verses are not present in the earliest complete manuscripts of Mark.

(49) Near death experiences (NDE) are just that; they are not total cessation of life.

(50) This may seem surprising to non-Jews since the sacred texts of Christianity dwell extensively on the afterlife.

(51) *The Jews in the Time of Jesus*, p.60

CHAPTER FOUR

(52) *Rescuing the Bible from Fundamentalism*, p.104

(53) If you recall from Chapter 2, Satan is an invention of the Zoroastrians that infiltrated the beliefs of the Jewish people. (See more on this in Chapter 5.)

(54) Although Christian theologians contend Acts was written by Luke, the general consensus among biblical scholars is that the writer was a Greek-speaking Gentile who supported Paul's cause. It is believed the book was written after Paul's death and is based primarily on oral tradition. Many scholars feel the author took creative license in his accounts of Paul's activities and the early church to help promote the cause of Christianity.

(55) Hyam Maccoby, *The Mythmaker: Paul and the Invention of Christianity* (NY, Harper & Row, 1986)

(56) *Rescuing the Bible from Fundamentalism*, p.99

(57) Benammi (pseud.), *Aspects of Jewish Life and Thought (Letters of Benammi)*, (NY, Bernard G. Richards Co., 1922)

(58) A scattering of Jewish communities located outside Palestine and formed after the Babylonian exile.

(59) *The Jews in the Time of Jesus*, p.75

(60) Internet article: "Jews believe that Jesus was not the messiah" <http://whatjewsbelieve.org/explanation3.html>

(61) Interestingly, Paul himself still observed the Mosaic law (Acts 21:24, 26), kept the Sabbath (Acts 13:14), and observed Jewish holidays (Acts 20:16).

(62) Timothy Freke and Peter Gandy, *The Jesus Mysteries: Was the "Original Jesus" a Pagan God?* (NY, Three Rivers Press, 1999), p.3

(63) *The Jesus Mysteries*, p.36

(64) *The Jesus Mysteries*, p.16

(65) *The Jesus Mysteries*, p.4

(66) Many of these traits have also been traced to the myth of Osiris-Dionysus (Ibid., p.5).

(67) Internet article: "Paul and the Mystery Religions" <http://30ce.com/mithras.htm>

(68) Internet article: "Mithras" <http://www.iranvision.com/mithras.html>

(69) Internet article: "Some Similarities Between Mithraism and Christianity" <http://ancienthistory.about.com/cs/godsreligion/a/mithraismxmas.htm>

(70) *The Jews in the Time of Jesus*, p. 61

(71) Internet article, "Original Sin, An Overview," <http://www.sullivan-county.com/z/original_sin2.htm>

(72) Internet article, "The Jewish View of Sin," <http://www.myjewishlearning.com/holidays/Jewish_Holidays/Yom_Kippur/Themes_and_Theology/Jewish_View_of_Sin.html>

(73) Internet article, "Jewish Views on Sin," <http://en.wikipedia.org/wiki/Jewish_views_on_sin>

(74) *The Jews in the Time of Jesus*, p.188

(75) Barrie Wilson, PhD., *How Jesus Became Christian* (NY, St. Martin's Press, 2008), p.255

CHAPTER FIVE

(76) Tyler F. Williams, Assistant Professor of Theology at The King's University College in Edmonton, Alberta, notes that virtually every modern English translation continues to render *ha-satan* as "Satan" in the book of Job, along with an accompanying footnote. He wonders why it isn't the other way around. <http://biblical-studies.ca/blog/2008/03/26/the-mysterious-appearance-of-satan-in-english-translations-of-the-book-of-job/>

(77) Elaine Pagels, *The Origin of Satan: How Christians Demonized Jews, Pagans, and Heretics* (NY, Random House, 1995), p.41

(78) There is considerable material available on the relationship between the morning star and "Lucifer;" however, space does not allow me to elaborate. I urge readers to do their own research.

(79) Origen is generally considered to be one of the greatest theologians in the early Christian movement. He is also called the most inventive diabologist of the entire Christian tradition by Jeffrey Burton Russell in *Satan: the Early Christian Tradition* (1987).

(80) Origen: De Principiis 1.5.5

(81) Internet article: "King of Tyre"
<http://assemblyoftrueisrael.com/Documents/Kingoftyre.html>

(82) Internet article: "The King of Tyre"
<http://www.concordant.org/expohtml/TheSpiritWorld/TheKingOfTyre.html>

(83) Origen, De Principiis, Book I, Chapter 5, Verse 4

(84) Paul Enns, *Moody Handbook of Theology*, (Chicago, Moody Press, 1989)

(85) Also known as the Greek Apocalypse (or Revelation) of Moses, Latin Life of Adam and Eve, Slavonic Life of Adam and Eve, and The Armenian Penitence of Adam. The actual date of the writing in unknown, but believed to be somewhere between 20 BCE to 70 CE.

(86) Internet source: "The Life of Adam and Eve, Serpent's Approach to Paradise (Armenian translation)," [44]17.2b,2c,
<http://www2.iath.virginia.edu/anderson/vita/tables/vita.table19.html>

(87) Justin Martyr is often cited as one of the most influential figures in early Christianity.

(88) Henry Ansgar Kelly, *Satan, A Biography* (NY, Cambridge University Press, 2006), p.176

(89) Early exegetes revered the authority of Augustine and few dared to challenge him directly (from Constructing Antichrist by Kevin L. Hughes, 2005, Google Books).

(90) *Ancient Christian Writings: St. Augustine, The Literal Meaning of Genesis, Vol. 2,* translated and annotated by John Hammond Taylor, SJ (Paulist Press, 1982), pp.135-136

(91) Internet source: "Serpents (symbolism)" <http://en.wikipedia.org/wiki/Serpent_(symbolism)>

(92) Mucalina, the king of snakes, shielded the Buddha from the elements as the Buddha sat in mediation.

(93) Using their vivid imaginations, it was these same writers that produced the literally hundreds of documents evidenced by the discovery of the Nag Hammadi codices in 1945 and the Dead Sea Scrolls between 1947 and 1956.

(94) T.J. Wray and Gregory Mobley, *The Birth of Satan: Tracing the Devil's Biblical Roots* (NY, Palgrave Macmillan, 2005), p.98

(95) Biblical scholars believe a number of people wrote the Book of Enoch over a period of about 260 years (c. 200 BCE to 50 CE). It is attributed to Enoch, the patriarch who "was no more because God took him." (Gen. 5:24)

(96) The dating of Jubilees has been somewhat problematic for biblical scholars. General consensus is that it was written between 160 to 140 BCE.

(97) Craig A. Evans, *Noncanonical Writings and New Testament Interpretation,* (Hendrickson Publishers, 1992) p. 23

(98) Cf. Daniel 4:13

(99) 1Enoch, 10:8,9

(100) An archangel

(101) 1Enoch 10:11-12

(102) Book of Jubilees, 10:8

(103) Jeffrey Burton Russell, *The Devil: Perceptions of Evil from Antiquity to Primitive Christianity* (New York, Cornell University Press, 1977), p.222, n.3

(104) "Does Satan Really Exist?," Our Baptist Heritage, 1993-Mar/Apr

(105) Norman Cohn, *Cosmos, Chaos and The World to Come* (New Haven and London, Yale University Press, 1993)

CHAPTER SIX

(106) Internet article, "Major Religions of the World Ranked by Number of Adherents" <http://www.adherents.com/Religions_By_Adherents.html adherents.com>

(107) Internet article, "Is Punishment in Hell Temporary or Eternal?" <http://www.religioustolerance.org/hel_eter.htm>

(108) Internet article, "Various Views of Hell: As Seen by Conservative Christians" <http://www.religioustolerance.org/hell_eva.htm>

(109) This was the teaching of the Egyptians, Zoroastrians, and Greco-Romans.

(110) Origen, third century theologian, taught that the unsaved are tortured in Hell temporarily, with a series of graded punishments, until they are sufficiently cleansed to be accepted into Heaven. This included Satan and his demons. Other early church fathers who agreed with this concept were Clements of Alexandria (150-215 CE), Gregory of Nazianzus (330-390 CE), and Gregory of Nyssa (335-390 CE).

(111) Some of the earliest descriptions of the underworld occur in myths from ancient Mesopotamia.

(112) Enoch 10:13 < http://www.sacred-texts.com/bib/boe/boe013.htm>

(113) Enoch 14:5 < http://www.sacred-texts.com/bib/boe/boe017.htm>

(114) Tertullian (c. 155-230 CE), noted second century theologian, has been credited in numerous places with the following statement: "At that greatest of all spectacles, that last and eternal judgment how shall I admire, how laugh, how rejoice, how exult, when I behold so many proud monarchs groaning in the lowest abyss of darkness; so many magistrates liquefying in … flames … philosophers blushing in red-hot fires …"

(115) Internet article, "What Did the Early Christians Believe About Hell?" <http://www.pleaseconvinceme.com/index/What_Did_the_Early_Christians_Believe_About_Hell>

(116) Internet article, "Hebrew Visions of Hell and Paradise: Revelation of Moses (A), Heaven, Hell, and Paradise," <http://www.sacred-texts.com/journals/jras/1893-15.htm>

(117) Biblical books included in the Vulgate and accepted in the Roman Catholic and Orthodox canon, but considered non-canonical by Protestants because they are not part of the Hebrew Scriptures. Protestants consider them useful but not "divinely inspired."

(118) Remember, during Jesus' time, the Gentiles had not yet been "grafted in" by Paul.

(119) Also called valley of the son of Hinnom and Valley of Ben Hinnom. Said to be located southwest of ancient Jerusalem, but the actual location is disputed.

(120) Quoted by Lloyd R. Bailey in "Gehenna: The Topography of Hell," Biblical Archaeologist 49/3 [1986], 188-89)

(121) Hermann L. Strack and Paul Billerbeck, *Kommentar zum Neuen Testament aus Talmud and Midrasch*, 5 vols. [Munich: Beck, 1922-56], 4:2:1030 (Wikipedia.org cited reference)

(122) Internet article, "The Fires of Gehenna: Views of Scholars" <http://blog.bibleplaces.com/2011/04/fires-of-gehenna-views-of-scholars.html>; See also "Was 'Gehenna' a Smoldering Garbage Dump?" <https://bbhchurchconnection.wordpress.com/2011/04/06/was-gehenna-a-smoldering-garbage-dump/>

(123) Thomas B. Thayer, *The Origin and History of the Doctrine of Endless Punishment*, (Boston, Universalist Publishing House, 1881)

(124) Howard Schwartz, *Tree of Souls: The Mythology of Judaism* (NY, Oxford University Press, 2004)

(125) According to Dr. Adam Clarke, British Methodist theologian and Biblical scholar (1760-1832), the word hell as used in the common translation conveys an improper meaning of the original word.

(126) "No biblical text authorizes the statement that the 'soul' is separated from the body at the moment of death." (The Interpreter's Dictionary of the Bible, 1962, Vol. 1, "Death"); "The belief that the soul continues its existence after the dissolution of the body is ... nowhere expressly taught in Holy Scripture ..." (Internet article, "Immortality of the Soul" <http://www.jewishencyclopedia.com/articles/8092-immortality-of-the-soul>

(127) Currently Professor Emeritus of History at the University of California, Santa Barbara.

(128) Internet article, "The Biblical Truth About the Immortal Soul" <http://www.ucg.org/booklet/heaven-and-hell-what-does-bible-really-teach/biblical-truth-about-immortal-soul/>

(129) Jerome (347-420 CE), the translator for the Vulgate, also believed in the immortality of the soul.

(130) I was unable to find any scriptural support for Mr. Graham's remarks.

(131) Internet article, "The Pagan Origin of the Doctrine of Hell" <http://www.godsplanforall.com/paganoriginofhell>

(132) C.L. Pinnock, "The Conditional View," in *Four Views of Hell*, editor, William Crockett (Grand Rapids, Zondervan, 1992), p. 148

CHAPTER SEVEN

(133) Internet articles, "2012: Six End-of-the-World Myths Debunked," news.nationalgeographic.com; "2012: Beginning of the End or Why the World Won't End?", NASA.gov

(134) If I were to pinpoint the reason for becoming a Christian, I would have to say it was the fear generated by this ominous book.

(135) Jonathan Kirsch, *A History of the End of the World*, (NY, HarperCollins, 2006), p. 157

(136) The title of a song made popular in the 1960's.

(137) Henry Bettenson and Chris Maunder, eds., *Documents of the Christian Church, 3rd ed.* (Oxford UP, 1999)

(138) Many bible scholars believe Domitian was the emperor that exiled John to the island of Patmos (where he wrote the book of Revelation).

(139) Nearly all New Testament scholars are certain Domitian is John's "beast from the sea" (See Revelation 13:1).

(140) It is interesting to note that John does not refer to Jesus by name as the rider of the white horse. In fact, in verse 12, he writes that the rider "has a name inscribed that no one knows but himself." Yet Christians have adopted the various titles John uses in this portion of scripture as alternate names for Jesus.

(141) Similar scriptures can be found in Mark 13 and Luke 21.

(142) Often viewed as the only 'authentic' bible.

(143) The kingdom of God (*malkut shaddai*) is specifically a Jewish term and is seen as the time when *Yahweh* will be universally recognized as the ruler over all the earth. It is said the author of Matthew was writing specifically to the Jews so he used the kingdom of Heaven (*malkut shamayim*) in deference to their practice of not using the name of "God."

(144) *A History of the End of the World*, p. 135

(145) Founder of the Seventh Day Adventists movement.

(146) President Reagan commented that the coup was a "sign that the day of Armageddon isn't far off. Everything's falling into place. It can't be long now." (Quoted by Grace Halsell, *Prophecy and Politics: Militant Evangelists on the Road to Nuclear War*, Laurence Hill & Company, CT, 1986, p. 45)

(147) The "catching up" of Christians in the air to meet Christ (1 Thessalonians 4:16-17).

(148) The word appears only one time in the bible (Revelation 16:16). So-called "experts" have been unable to agree on its actual

location, but popular writers and preachers believe it to be in northern Israel.

(149) Although this saying is often attributed to Charles Schulz, creator of "Peanuts," the Charles M. Schulz Museum states Mr. Schulz made no such statement. (Source: Snopes.com).

CHAPTER EIGHT

(150) In fact, the word "Antichrist" (capitalized) does not appear anywhere in the bible or for that matter, in any of the apocalyptic literature.

(151) According to the International Standard Bible, Paul was specifically writing about Caligula (37-41 CE), the "mad emperor" in power during the time of his epistle.

(152) Traditionally believed to be written by the same person who wrote the Gospel of John and Revelation, but many modern scholars challenge this view.

(153) Although numerous other bible scriptures are taken literally, John's use of the "last hour" is nearly always considered figurative and considered to be relevant today, two millennia later.

(154) Robert Fuller, *Naming the Antichrist: The History of an American Obsession* (Oxford University Press, 1995), p. 21

(155) Letter to the Philadelphians, 7:1 (135 CE)

(156) Gregory Charles Jenks, *The Origins & Early Development of the Antichrist Myth*, (Walter de Gruyter, 1991), p.31

(157) Jeffrey Burton Russell, *Satan: The Early Christian Tradition*, (Cornell University Press, 1987) p. 88

(158) Bernard McGinn, *The Antichrist: Two Thousand Years of the Human Fascination with Evil* (NY, Columbia University Press, 2000)

(159) Internet article, "Prophesies of the Antichrist by Early Church Fathers,"
<http://www.unitypublishing.com/prophecy/AntichristbySaints.htm>

(160) William C. Weinrich, "Antichrist in the Early Church," Concordia Theological Quarterly, Vol. 49, Numbers 2 and 3, April-July 1985

(161) Internet article, "Letter on the Origin and Time of the Antichrist," <http://www.pbs.org/wgbh/pages/frontline/shows/apocalypse/primary/adsoletter.html>

(162) First mentioned in the book of Daniel (9:27, 11:31, 12:11). Also found in Matthew 24:15 and Mark 13:14. Most modern bible scholars believe this term describes the actions of the Seleucid king, Antiochus IV Epiphanes, who reigned in the mid-second century BCE (see Chapter Two). Futurists believe it refers to an end-time act of the Antichrist.

(163) *Fiber Optics: The Eye of the Antichrist*, referenced in Naming the Antichrist, p. 181

CHAPTER NINE

(164) See Dr. Craig's Q&A on "Personal God" <http://www.ReasonableFaith.org/personal-god>

(165) Internet article, "Anthropomorphism, Anthropomorphites," <http://www.newadvent.org/cathen/01558c.htm>

(166) Rick Warren, evangelical mega-pastor, is quoted in an interview as saying, "Jesus is God. My God is Jesus." (See religionnews.com/blogs/mark-silk/different-abrahamic-gods)

(167) Tillich called it the "shock of nonbeing."

(168) The most prominent god in many early societies was the sun god, who took many forms and went by many names.

(169) According to John Shelby Spong, author and retired bishop of the Episcopal Church USA, even today religion is primarily a search for security -- a way to stave off anxiety over the unknown.

(170) Internet article, "Origins of Religion," <http://www.fsmitha.com/h1/ch00.htm>

(171) Internet article, "God—A Quest," <http://www.lifepositive.com/spirit/god/concept-of-god.asp>

(172) Internet article, "Lost Goddesses Writing Found," <http://www.goddesses.com>

(173) There were other nomadic invaders as well. The most famous were the Semitic people (the Hebrews) who came from the deserts of the south and invaded Canaan.

(174) To the early Mesopotamians, the goddess *Nammu* (sea) was the "the mother who gave birth to heaven and earth."

(175) See menu item "Browse the Pantheons," <http://www.godchecker.com>

(176) Internet source: "Monotheism" <http://www.newworldencyclopedia.org/entry/Monotheism>

(177) After the death of Akhenaten, this god fell into obscurity and the people returned to their many-god ideology.

(178) The Israelites were also guilty of "henotheism" (belief and worship of a single god while accepting the existence or possible existence of other deities).

(179) Many would be shocked to learn there is archeological evidence indicating the early Israelites also worshipped the "wife" of *Yahweh*, a fertility goddess named Asherah (aka Astarte and Istar). Pottery found in the Sinai desert includes inscriptions that show *Yahweh* and Asherah were worshipped as a pair. Some scholars believe the mention of "queen of heaven" in the Hebrew Bible refers to Asherah. See *"Did God Have a Wife?"* by William G. Dever, an American archaeologist, specializing in the history of Israel.

(180) Something that baffles understanding and cannot be explained.

(181) Although the actual word is not used, some Christian apologists believe the core aspect of the trinity is interwoven in scripture and have offered various "proofs" to support this theory. Other scholars believe the original Hebrew language does not denote a "uni-plural" god and it is not until the Greek scriptures (New Testament) that the idea of the trinity develops.

(182) To Autolycus 2:15

(183) A profession of faith used within the Christian liturgy of some churches.

(184) See complete text of creed at http://www.churches.kconline.com/all_saints/creeds.htm#athanasian.

(185) Hinduism teaches that although the Hindu trinity gods appear to be sovereign and different, in reality they are all aspects of the Supreme God.

(186) Some would contend they believe in God because the complexity of our planet points to a deliberate Designer. However, I believe this thinking is "after the fact" and the core reason people need/want a god in their life is directly related to Paul Tillech's theory ("existential angst").

(187) To lapse or fall backwards in one's relationship with God; to lose interest in following the Lord.

www.ingramcontent.com/pod-product-compliance
Lightning Source LLC
Chambersburg PA
CBHW071503040426
42444CB00008B/1466